CAMBRIDGE LIBRARY COLLECTION

Books of enduring scholarly value

Travel and Exploration

The history of travel writing dates back to the Bible, Caesar, the Vikings and the Crusaders, and its many themes include war, trade, science and recreation. Explorers from Columbus to Cook charted lands not previously visited by Western travellers, and were followed by merchants, missionaries, and colonists, who wrote accounts of their experiences. The development of steam power in the nineteenth century provided opportunities for increasing numbers of 'ordinary' people to travel further, more economically, and more safely, and resulted in great enthusiasm for travel writing among the reading public. Works included in this series range from first-hand descriptions of previously unrecorded places, to literary accounts of the strange habits of foreigners, to examples of the burgeoning numbers of guidebooks produced to satisfy the needs of a new kind of traveller - the tourist.

Across Thibet

The French explorer, author and legislator Gabriel Bonvalot (1853–1933) travelled widely in Central Asia in the 1880s. This two-volume English translation by C.B. Pitman of the 1889–90 French original was published in 1891. It describes Bonvalot's expedition across Europe and Asia to French Indochina. Accompanied by Prince Henri d'Orléans whose father, the duc de Chartres, financed the expedition, Bonvalot left Paris in July 1889. In Volume 1, the expedition crosses first Russia and then Siberia, making its way south to Tibet. The obstacles encountered are considerable, with temperatures reaching 40 degrees below zero (Bonvalot describes how the fat that the expedition eats for butter is so hard that it may be 'used as a projectile') and altitude sickness affecting many of the party. The volume ends as the party enters Tibet, but without being certain exactly where they are.

T0371373

Cambridge University Press has long been a pioneer in the reissuing of out-of-print titles from its own backlist, producing digital reprints of books that are still sought after by scholars and students but could not be reprinted economically using traditional technology. The Cambridge Library Collection extends this activity to a wider range of books which are still of importance to researchers and professionals, either for the source material they contain, or as landmarks in the history of their academic discipline.

Drawing from the world-renowned collections in the Cambridge University Library and other partner libraries, and guided by the advice of experts in each subject area, Cambridge University Press is using state-of-the-art scanning machines in its own Printing House to capture the content of each book selected for inclusion. The files are processed to give a consistently clear, crisp image, and the books finished to the high quality standard for which the Press is recognised around the world. The latest print-on-demand technology ensures that the books will remain available indefinitely, and that orders for single or multiple copies can quickly be supplied.

The Cambridge Library Collection brings back to life books of enduring scholarly value (including out-of-copyright works originally issued by other publishers) across a wide range of disciplines in the humanities and social sciences and in science and technology.

Across Thibet

Being a Translation of
De Paris au Tonkin à travers le Tibet inconnu

VOLUME 1

GABRIEL BONVALOT

CAMBRIDGE UNIVERSITY PRESS

Cambridge, New York, Melbourne, Madrid, Cape Town,
Singapore, São Paolo, Delhi, Mexico City

Published in the United States of America by Cambridge University Press, New York

www.cambridge.org
Information on this title: www.cambridge.org/9781108046336

This edition first published 1891
This digitally printed version 2012

ISBN 978-1-108-04633-6 Paperback

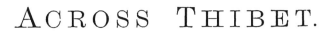

ACROSS THIBET.

M. BONVALOT AND PRINCE HENRY OF ORLEANS.

ACROSS THIBET.

BEING A TRANSLATION OF

"DE PARIS AU TONKIN À TRAVERS LE TIBET INCONNU,"

BY

GABRIEL BONVALOT.

With Illustrations from Photographs taken by Prince Henry of Orleans, and Map of Route.

TRANSLATED BY C. B. PITMAN.

Vol. I.

CASSELL & COMPANY, Limited:

LONDON, PARIS & MELBOURNE.

1891.

TRANSLATOR'S PREFACE.

THE last journey undertaken by M. Bonvalot, who was on this occasion accompanied by Prince Henry of Orleans, the eldest son of the Duc de Chartres, has, perhaps, excited even greater interest than the preceding one, when, together with two other Frenchmen, he accomplished the difficult if not unprecedented feat of reaching India by scaling those tablelands of the Pamir—the "roof of the world," as that mountain mass is often called—concerning which there is so much talk just now. M. Bonvalot entitled that book, "Aux Indes par terre," or, to give it the English title which I adopted as an equivalent, "Through the Heart of Asia." It was a laborious and even dangerous journey, bringing out those qualities of courage, self-command, tenacity, knowledge of human character, and good-humour, which go to make up the successful traveller and explorer. It is to the possession of all these qualities that he undoubtedly owes the renown which he has achieved as a traveller, and I do not think it will be possible for anyone to read the following pages without being impressed with the fact that M. Bonvalot—who was evidently well seconded by his two companions, Prince Henry and the Belgian missionary Father Dedeken—is not only a man of dauntless pluck, but a keen observer of men. If he has not that undue and self-depreciating modesty which is but pride in another form, he does not in any way boast of his exploits; but one has only to read his dispassionate and almost bare record of the temperature and the privations of the months spent on the highlands of Thibet to realise what the chilling cold and the wasting miseries of that terrible winter must have been.

Yet all this is related in as matter-of-fact a tone as if the writer were describing a journey to Cairo or some other well-known place in touch with civilisation. Starting from the frontiers of Siberia, and coming out at the other end of Asia, on the coast of the new French colony of Tonquin, M. Bonvalot and his companions not only traversed that portion of Thibet which several English travellers, such as Dalgleish and Carey, and the great Russian Prjevalsky, had explored, but going beyond the limits which their predecessors had reached, forced their way over the tablelands and came out on the other side, this journey being one which no European had ever accomplished; the only persons who had trodden the same paths being the Thibetans on their way to and from the holy city of Lhassa. Although they encountered many obstacles, and must at times have been in considerable peril, they met with no active hostility worth the name, so that the narrative of their journey is not a sensational one.

In translating the book into English, I have endeavoured to remain as far as possible true to the original meaning; but as the work is a very large one, I have taken it upon myself to omit certain passages—chiefly of dialogue, especially in the chapters relating to countries where other travellers had been before. The list of the collections which the explorers brought back with them has also been omitted in this edition, these collections having been exhibited in the Paris Natural History Museum, and not being destined for England. Pains have been taken to reduce to uniformity many place-names which in the original are given in a variety of forms, but in not a few instances the text furnishes no data for determining whether the names are those of different or of the same places, and in such cases there was no option but to follow the original. I may add that the figures relating to the temperature have been altered to the Fahrenheit scale throughout.

C. B. PITMAN.

CONTENTS OF VOL. I.

—◆—

A*

CHAPTER VI.

STRIKING THE SOUTHERN ROUTE.

CHAPTER VII.

A DEATH IN THE CARAVAN.

CHAPTER VIII.

A WILDERNESS OF MOUNTAINS.

LIST OF ILLUSTRATIONS IN VOL. I.

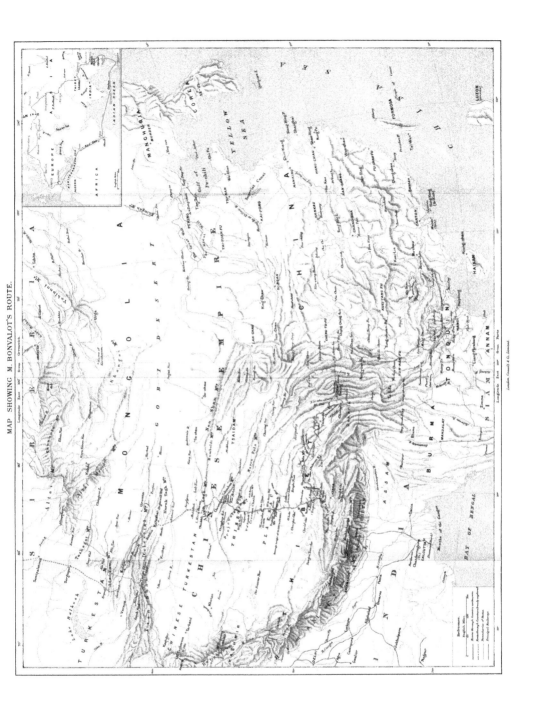

MAP SHOWING M. BONVALOT'S ROUTE.

The material originally positioned here is too large for reproduction in this reissue. A PDF can be downloaded from the web address given on page iv of this book, by clicking on 'Resources Available'.

ACROSS THIBET.

CHAPTER I.

AMONG THE LAMAS.

How the Journey was Suggested—Rachmed—At Moscow—Through the Ural Mountains—
Arrival at Djarkent—Organising the Caravan—At Kuldja—Father Dedeken—Abdullah,
the Interpreter—Across the Tien Shan—In the Province of Ili—Kirghis and Kalmucks
—Chinese Justice—The River Kunges—Mongols—Exposing the Dead—Visit to a Grand
Lama—A Lama Monastery and Pagoda—Timurlik—Kirghis Immigrants—Valley of the
Tsakma—The Joy of the Desert.

RACHMED.

OF the first half of my route from Paris
to Tonquin through Thibet I do not
propose to say anything, because it is
already pretty well known, and because
I have described it briefly in a volume
published about eight years ago. I shall
also pass with rapid strides over the
route which the travellers Prjevalsky and
Carey traversed before us, speaking more
in detail of the regions we were the
first to explore.

It used to be the fashion to invoke
the muses before one began to write a narrative, but all that is
out of date; and for my own part I would simply entreat the
cross-grained rheumatics and treacherous fever to be so kind as
to let me keep my word with my publisher, and write with
as little delay as possible the story of a journey which I undertook with great pleasure, but which, as I must frankly admit,
it is much less agreeable to put upon paper.

In January, 1889, we were talking, at the house of my

1

good friend Henri Lorin, as he reminded me upon my return last winter, about travel and exploration, and he asked me if I had any fresh project in view. I told him that a very interesting journey would be one from Paris to Tonquin overland, cutting out a route of one's own across the whole of Asia. And when he asked me to indicate my probable itinerary upon the map, I drew a line through Chinese Turkestan, the higher tablelands of Thibet, and the valleys of the great rivers of China and of the Indo-Chinese peninsula. Those who were looking over my shoulder thought this scheme a splendid one; but, for my own part, still feeling the effects of my journey over the Pamir, I would not allow myself to think of putting it into execution, for the good reason that when I let my fancy turn to travel, I am sure to be carried away by it.

A few months later, on coming back from the Exhibition, where I had been to catch a glimpse, as it were, of the distant lands in which I had wandered, this same friend wrote to say that there was a person desirous of travelling with me in Asia. The first thing to ascertain was whether it was someone prepared to follow me blindfold, for my intention was not to play the globe-trotter, but to explore. I was told that this was so, and, forgetting all about my resolve to take a rest, I plunged into the study of the narratives of Father Huc and Prjevalsky.

Little time was lost in coming to an understanding with the Duc de Chartres, who offered to participate in the expenses of an exploring expedition in which his son was to take part. We at once agreed that our undertaking should be a national one, and that the collections we might make should be handed over to our Museums. My future companion, Prince Henry of Orleans, was delighted at the plan which I submitted to him, though it was a somewhat vague one, for travelling has this much in common with war, that, before getting upon the ground, it is idle to commit oneself to any positive arrangements.

The preliminary preparations having been rapidly completed, we left Paris on the 6th of July, just when Paris was in the full fever of her Exhibition. At Moscow, we were to be joined by Rachmed, my faithful companion during my two previous journeys, he having been found out for me in the Caucasus at the place where I had expected he would be, for I know where Rachmed prefers to live when he is not on the tramp. The worthy fellow was preparing to come to the Exhibition, by way of realising a dream he had for some time been cherishing; his ticket had been taken, and he was about to embark at Batoum, when he got my telegram, saying that if he cared to come to China with me, he was to go and wait for me at Moscow. So he went and changed his ticket for one to Moscow, not in the best of humours, for it cost him a pang not to see the Exhibition. Still he did not hesitate, being afraid, as he confided to one of my friends, of forfeiting my regard. Rachmed is an Uzbeg by birth, and belongs to one of the branches of that fine Turkish race which, as I am never tired of repeating, comprises so many noble specimens of humanity.

In Russia we were treated most handsomely, and furnished with all necessary letters of recommendation to the Consuls along the Chinese frontier. Remaining at Moscow only long enough to make the many necessary purchases, we just stopped at Nijni-Novgorod, went down the Volga, ascended the Kama, and traversed the Ural chain of mountains. At Tiumen we again took boat, and landed at Omsk, whence, after making some purchases, we started again for Semipalatinsk, where we purchased the European goods which we were afraid of not being able to get at the frontier itself, and, after being very much jolted in a *tarantass*, arrived at Djarkent, the last town on Russian territory.

Before entering China, we had to organise our caravan and recruit the staff needful for carrying out our project, but I will spare the reader an enumeration of the details and trouble entailed by these preliminaries of an exploring party. Let me, however, say that the thorough organisation of a caravan for a journey which is to end Heaven knows when or where, is the most difficult part of an explorer's work. In the Asiatic countries we were about to traverse, vehicles are not used, and the rivers are not navigable, being obstacles instead of means of communication as they are elsewhere. It is imperative, therefore, neither to forget anything nor to take a single superfluous article. So one tries to think of everything, and to foresee all contingencies ; but, after having eliminated as much as possible, it is astonishing to find how heavy the load is.

Meanwhile, we had to recruit our men at Djarkent on the frontier of Siberia. This was most difficult, for here we could only secure men very much below the mark, and not at all built for a long journey. Rachmed inspected them first, and, in presenting them to me, his unvarying observation was, " They are of no use for the road." I could see that he was right. There was not one of them who had respectable antecedents ; they were a pack of lazy and penniless fellows who were anxious only to get across the frontier in our wake. Among them there is not one of those adventurers, vigorous and ready for anything, who have already looked death in the face, and would go through fire after the leader whom chance had given them, provided that leader had succeeded in attaching them to himself by a mixture of good and of bad usage. How much we regretted not having our base of operations in Russian Turkestan—at Samarkand, for instance, where there is no lack of good men. It is true we had three Russians who would suit us very well, but they made it a condition, when they took service with us, that they should not go beyond the Lob Nor.

September 6.—We left Djarkent on the 2nd, and, marching by short stages, reached Kuldja to-day, and were most hospitably

FATHER DEDEKEN.

received by the Russian Consul and his secretary. We spend a few hours very pleasantly with the members of the Belgian mission, one of whom, Father Dedeken, has completed his engagement, and is about to return to Europe. As he has an appointment at Shanghai, he will go with us to the coast, and perhaps accompany us to Europe. He speaks Chinese, and as he is a man of strong will, we are glad to have our party reinforced by him.   His Chinese servant, Bartholomeus, who is to accompany him, is honest—which few Chinese servants appear to be—but very obstinate, which, on the contrary, seems to be very common in China.

Prince Henry, Father Dedeken, Rachmed, Bartholomeus, and myself form the nucleus of the expedition.   We have, too, an interpreter named Abdullah, who speaks Chinese and Mongolian, and who accompanied the celebrated Prjevalsky.   He seems to be an honest sort of fellow, but his vanity, his boastfulness, his talkativeness make us very uneasy.

His account of what he went through in the Tsaïdam alarms our followers, and he seems bent upon dissuading us from undertaking anything out of the beaten tracks.   It must be added that the Russian Consul at Kuldja is not much more encouraging, and when Prince Henry tells him we are going to try to reach Batang, he smiles incredulously, and advises him not to be lured on by that idea.   He points out to us that we have no escort, no felt tent, no Chinese passport.   But experience has taught us that one can get on without either of these three things which he regards as indispensable.   As regards the passport, I must say that the main cause of our success was our omission to give notice of our journey to the Tsong li Yamen at Pekin.   By asking for a passport to travel in those parts of China which have been little visited, we should have excited the attention of Chinese diplomacy   The mandarins would have given us the warmest letters of recommendation, and then, as soon as our itinerary was known, would have sent orders for every sort of means to be used to stop us on the road, and compel us to turn back.   Such has been the lot of all travellers in China, from the late Prjevalsky down to Richthofen, Count Bela-Szechny, and so many others who have been stopped in their journeys by various devices.

After having completed our caravan as best we could at Kuldja, all we wanted, in order to continue our journey, was the authorisation of the Chinese governor of the province. This was granted us after a visit in which etiquette was very carefully observed, insomuch that we were offered three cups of tea and a bottle of champagne ; and the Governor gave us two safe-conducts to take us to the frontiers of the province of Ili.

September 12.—To-day the small European colony kindly escorts us to the gate of the town, and cordially wishes us a safe journey and happy return home.

And so at last we find ourselves in the saddle. We first make in an easterly direction, but change our course as soon as we have crossed the Tien Shan, as it is Tonquin that we have in view. Shall we ever get there, and if so, by what route? There is all the old continent to cross, the least known portion of China, Thibet and its highlands, the deserts, and the deep rivers, to say nothing of the human beings who look upon every stranger as an enemy. All this I might have said to myself, and to these reflections might have added that we were only five or six to face an unknown situation, before which so many others better equipped and prepared had quailed. But I must confess that I had not one of these rhetorical thoughts in my head when once I found myself fairly started, abandoning myself to the pleasure of being in the open and looking about me with the eager curiosity of the traveller whose eyes, almost starting from their orbits, scan the horizon like a hungry hawk in search of prey.

After getting quit of the dust which reminds me of Turkestan, the soil, the landscape, and the cultivation of the plain recall the neighbourhood of Samarkand and Tashkend. The beardless faces, the sunken eyes, and the long dresses of the men show that one is in China. The fertility of the valley of Ili is remarkable, so that for the last few years its population has been growing very rapidly. A great many of the Tarantshis who had fled to Russian territory are coming back to the places which their forefathers had cultivated, and a number of emigrants come from Kashgar, and even from Eastern China; but it will be a long time before the inhabitants are numerous enough to cultivate to the full extent this region, which would feed hundreds of thousands.

Leaving the valley of Ili to our right, as far as Mazar, built upon an affluent of the Kash, we followed a very good road, frequently coming upon villages which have been abandoned by the Tarantshis, who, having taken part in the massacre of the Chinese, fled when the province of Ili was transferred from Russia to China. The houses are falling into ruins, and are gradually disappearing amid a growth of willows, poplars, and vines; weeds choke up the gardens; the irrigating canals are dried up, and the fields are fallow. Deserted though the soil is, however, it has not ceased to be generous; it is arrayed in verdure, and its aspect is bright and cheerful.

One of our men recognises the house in which he was born.

THE CARAVAN ON THE MARCH.

The roof has fallen in, the door has been carried off—for fuel no doubt—the walls are all cracked, and there are patches of barley growing at the extremity of the hearthstone. The Tarantshi was overcome with grief at the sight of the place all in ruins, and recalled how happily he had lived there with his parents, what fine crops they grew, and how cheap the food was.

I asked him why he had not remained there.

" We killed too many Chinese, Solons, and Sibos," he replied, " and upon the Chinese returning we fled."

" Now that you have crossed the frontier, will you return to Djarkent ? "

" Heaven preserve me, no! The soil is not good, and water is scarce. I shall go to Kashgar, where the family of one of my wives lives."

" Were you not married at Djarkent ? '

" Yes, and I had a child as well. He died the day before I came to offer you my services, and I gave my wife back to her father. I am quite free."

The facility with which this Mussulman abandoned his wife surprised me, but in this country it appears to be quite common.

What this Tarantshi told me about Ili was repeated to me by many others. Most of those who live in Russian territory are on the look-out for a chance of slipping across the frontier. The Chinese mandarins have the wit to entice them ; they do not ask them for papers. They let them settle on the uncultivated lands, and do not bother them about the past.

In the province of Ili, beyond Mazar, we meet a great many Siberian Kirghis, whom the excellence of the pasturages along the affluents of the Ili has attracted. They have kept the chiefs whom they had elected being Russian subjects. By order of the Chinese mandarin, and with the assent of the tribes, these chiefs will transmit their powers to their descendants.

Side by side with these very wealthy Kirghis we see some

2

very poor Kalmucks. The rich pastures and flocks belong to the former, while the latter are relegated to the less fertile tracts, which they cultivate without gaining a sufficiency. These Kalmucks are certainly not taking in appearance. They are frail, badly fed, badly housed, badly clad, and have a placid rather than an energetic and intelligent air. Nevertheless, they have for some time been entrusted with the defence of the country, and they must not leave the place assigned to them without asking permission from their chief. They are not only bound to the soil, but are liable to be requisitioned for police or orderly duty, and must have in readiness the sabre, the flint-lock gun, or the bow. Their "banners," to the number of twenty, distributed over the Tien Shan, play more or less the same part as those families which in Austria were established in the south of the empire in the region of the "military frontiers," as they were styled. Their neighbours do not appear to hold them in high esteem, for a Kirghis to whom I observed how mild a physiognomy these Mongols have, replied with a laugh—

"That is true. They are as mild as cows."

"In what way?"

"Because they can be milked without any trouble."

It appears that the Kirghis, who are daring, well armed, and unscrupulous, do not think twice about cheating and pillaging these Mongols. As the plunderers are Mussulmans, they can easily settle matters with their consciences, seeing that the victims are Buddhists, that is to say, people who have no "book," neither a Bible nor a Koran, and so are of no account.

The Chinese authorities intervene but rarely to mete out justice to those who are aggrieved; the offenders are nearly always out of reach in the mountains, where they find it so easy to hide, and then again it is easy, in this case, to obtain from their family or tribe either a tax which may be in arrears or a present which in ordinary times would be withheld. But when brigandage has reached such a point that there is no sort of security, the authorities resort to a ruse. By dint of promises and fair words, the chief who is the instigator of the trouble is enticed into the town and got rid of in some way or other. For instance, he is put into a cage between two impaling poles, and, by way of warning to offenders, he is left to die in this horrible posture. Sometimes it is a week before his agony ends in death. Having lost their leader the nomads are thrown more or less into confusion, and advantage is taken of this to obtain some kind of submission.

The Chinese authorities have succeeded in embodying a certain number of Kirghis, in registering them, so to speak. Thus we observed that the horsemen whom we meet wear round the neck a small tablet in a felt bag. When I ask what that means, I am told that for some time past every Kirghis who is going into the town must first appear before his leader and ask him for one of these tablets, upon which his name is written in Turkish, in Chinese, and in Mongolian. It is a passport which enables him to move about freely in the bazaars, and if in times of disturbance he should be caught without it he is arrested by the Chinese soldiers and visited with the most terrible punishments. On returning to his tribe, the traveller has to return the passport to his chief, and in this way it is possible to ascertain who are absent, and to exercise some sort of police control in the mountains. These men, riding about with the tablet flapping against their chest, enable one to realise the enormous power of an administration when opposed to the weakness of private interests without cohesion. The Chinese authorities have succeeded by dint of patience in getting the whip hand of these nomads, who used to make mock of them, and have put the yoke of the law upon their necks.

September 15.—To-day we left Mazar, and if the bridge over the Kash had not been carried away by a storm, we should have crossed that river so as to reach the valley of the Kunges by a neighbouring pass. But we were compelled to cross the mountain further north and find out a ferry higher up the river. After having climbed up and then followed the undulations of the uncultivated hills, we descried the valley, a sort of terrace at the foot of the mountains, a greyish steppe dotted over with a few tents and nomad flocks. It is commanded to the east by a chain of mountains more elevated than that to the north, and the slopes of which seem to us quite bare, while the summits are not white with snow.

The banks of the river present a somewhat attractive appearance, the stream flowing along like a ribbon amid verdure formed by poplars, willows, tamarisks which still bear a few flowers, liquorice-plants, barberries, and wild raspberries. There is abundance of water, and the grass is thick wherever the river reaches, while pheasants swarm in the undergrowth.

Passing a deserted village, we cross the small stream of Nilka and leave the marshy valley for the high plateau which overhangs it. In the midst of tall grass we come here and there upon cleared plots where the Mongols have their felt tents, which are smaller than those of the Kirghis, lower and more pointed at the summit. These Mongols are busy threshing the wheat in the open air, in the same way as other primitive peoples who do not employ any machine. A pole is put into the ground in the centre of the wheat, which is laid out upon the ground, and oxen are tied to this pole and made to tramp round in a line, children driving them along with a stick. These children are stark naked, and very weakly in appearance. Their stomachs are protuberant, and their skin, exposed constantly to the sun, is nearly black, while it seems to be merely thrown loosely over their frame, and to be about to come off whenever they raise their arms and cause their angular shoulder-blades to protrude.

September 16.—This evening we reach the banks of the

river, which is at least 650 feet wide at the point where we are to cross it, for it branches out and forms numerous small islands,

A LAMA DOCTOR (*p.* 15).

while the current is very impetuous. We hope that in the morning, when the water is lowest, we shall get our caravan over without mishap before sunrise. From our bivouac we can distinguish to the north white specks in the plain, at the foot of the mountains. These, it appears, are the tents of the lamas engaged upon the harvest; and when it is over, they will return to winter in the monastery built upon the left bank of the river.

We are now in a Buddhist country, in a land where the people believe in the transmigration of the soul from one body to another. This does not tend to respect for the human body or to regard for the dead. While walking through the reed-beds in search of small birds for our natural history collection, my foot comes into contact with the upper part of a human skull. It is quite white, stripped cleaner than could have been done by the cleverest medical student. Upon examining it, I find that it was the very image of the Kirghis skulls which I have had in my hand in Turkestan, there being the same depression of the occiput, the same breadth of cheek, the same prominent eyebrows, the same protruding cheek-bones, but with the forehead apparently less developed and rather lower, though quite as receding. We may assume that this skull was that of a man who did not possess any very marked intelligence, who was short in stature—as I learnt from the thigh-bone, which I picked up a little further—and who had excellent teeth, as is proved by a fragment of his lower jaw. The bits of clothing hanging from the thorn-bushes show that he was not a man of wealth. This was the place where his remains were exposed as soon as the soul had passed into a better body. Four stakes, with bits of stuff at the end of them, indicated that the corpse was deposited there, and the wild beasts, the birds of prey, and no doubt the dogs from the adjoining tents, have cleared away the terrestrial envelope of this Mongol, devouring his flesh and grinding his bones, and then time and the weather completed the work of destruction. There remain only a whitened skull, a half-gnawed thigh-bone, and a fragment of jaw; the soul has taken its flight, and the bits of stuff at the end of the stakes are praying for it, for, inscribed in black letters upon a yellow ground, are marvellous supplications brought from Lhassa.

September 17.—To-day, as we were certain of being able to overtake our caravan, which will be delayed in its progress by having to cross the ferry, we paid a visit to the Grand Lama, the head of the monastery. Our approach to the tents was heralded by the furious barking of some splendid long-haired dogs. The noise brings out the lamas, young and old, who drive away the angry mastiffs by throwing stones at them. We explain the object of our visit to the oldest of them, and he sends on in advance two young monks, and himself conducts us to the residence of his superior. The person who acts as our cicerone has an enormous head, a rather long neck, small eyes, and a big face covered with warts, so that his physiognomy would not be very pleasing but for the mouth and the smile playing upon his thick lips. It appears that this worthy man, whose age it would be very difficult to guess, is a celebrated doctor. His headdress is a greasy leather cap surmounted with a tuft, a small cap such as might fit a chorister boy, and which is much too small for so huge a head, upon which it produces much the same effect as would a wafer on the top of an orange. For dress he has a long serge robe coming down to the feet and fastened round the waist with a belt, while his small feet are encased in untanned leather, which does duty at once as stocking and as boot.

The Grand Lama received us very affably at the entrance to his tent of white felt, which was larger than any of the others. He himself drew aside the curtain, and invited us into his residence; and we, as soon as we had entered, seated ourselves in Eastern fashion to the left of the aperture. The yellow-looking little man asked us as to our health, offered us the services of his doctor, and talked to us in the most paternal and friendly tone. Leaving our interpreter to answer for us, we proceeded to inspect at our ease, but with due discretion, this incarnation of Buddha and his abode.

The Grand Lama appears to be about sixty. Like all the priests of his creed, he wears his hair short, and being beardless by nature, he has no need to shave. His features are regular, especially by comparison with those of his doctor. He has rather a broad face, but the black eyes are very intelligent, the mouth is delicate, and the eyelids very clearly defined. He is easy in his gestures, and has a good deal of unction in his voice. I should not be at all surprised if he ruled the fraternity excellently, for he gives the impression of being a man of mark. From time to time he takes a pinch of red snuff, which he puts out on to the nail of his thumb from an oval jade bottle with a silver stopper. He takes care that we are served with some tea with butter in it, which is the favourite drink of the Mongols and the Thibetans, and which I found very much to my liking upon tasting it for the first time.

Behind my host there stands upon a slab a gilt statue, which represents the Grand Lama of Lhassa. The Grand Lama seems to be very like him, and has the same smiling physiognomy.

There is nothing in the tent which indicates any effort at cleanliness or luxury. The whole of the furniture seems to be about equally neglected, and the only apparent value possessed by anything is a row of small jade vases placed upon a coffer covered with some yellow material opposite to the entrance; an altar has been raised, and some sacred images are enclosed in a sort of tabernacle or movable chapel, the shape of which reminds me of those I have seen in Italy; and, as is the case in Italy and also in Spain, these sacred images of Buddha are carried to the residences of such persons as ask for them, in order to facilitate their cure, which the doctor also helps to effect by means of remedies that have received the priestly benediction. Among these remedies are some truly extraordinary ones, of so singular an origin that I dare not explain them, for fear of being considered improper.

Presently there is a great noise of drums and cymbals, which is the call to prayer. So we take leave of the Grand Lama, who

THE TIEN SHAN MOUNTAINS.

rises, offers us his hand, and wishes us a safe journey, with the same smiling face which is seen alike in the Buddhas of statues and in the Buddhas of flesh and blood. The aged priest readily gives us permission to visit the pagoda built close to the winter monastery.

As we go out we notice the cymbal-players, who are standing in front of a large tent which is used for religious service during the harvest. The lamas are nearly all out in the fields, and the number of worshippers is very small, the congregation consisting mainly of youths with skull-caps on their clean-shaven heads, and a long monkish robe fastened round the waist with a belt.

3

The monastery consists of a congeries of houses in the Mongol style, forming a square. Nothing can be simpler than the architecture of these buildings: four walls, a door, a window, a fireplace, a hole in the ceiling, some forage on the roof, and that is about all. As far as we can judge by what can be seen through the chinks in the closed doors, the furniture is not worth speaking of, for we can see only a few chests, some clothing, and a certain quantity of tools. Moreover, the lamas, faithful to their nomad habits, are said to inhabit, even during the cold season, their felt tents, erected in the courtyards formed by these dwellings. They are built of earth, rubble, and wood, and are used as much for cattle as for human beings.

The pagoda is new, and its walls are whitewashed. The main door being open, we enter into a sort of rectangular barn. The first thing which strikes the eye is the altar, upon which are burning lamps whose flame sheds a glow upon the gilding of the statues. One represents Buddha in his youth, wreathed in smiles and seated upon a throne. Behind him a lama, in gilt metal, is smiling as amiably as Buddha himself. Like him, he has long ears—the better to hear prayer, no doubt; and he hold his hands out, one against the other, in the attitude of a person ready to applaud, while at the same time maintaining an aspect of great dignity.

Beside the high altar, in a chapel of more modest proportions, is the statue of a person dressed in yellow, with an apron on the knees and a chaplet in the hand. He, we are told, is to be the successor of the Grand Lama, and his functions are analogous to those of a Christian saint, he having to intercede for the faithful and to transmit their prayers to the proper destination. On the table of the altar are a number of small cups containing oil, and, beside these, there are bronze ewers, bells, bundles of images, peacocks' feathers disposed as trophies, packets of sacred books and printed prayers, phials containing grains or perfumes, and other trifles, which are, nevertheless, of high value, for they have been brought from the holy city of Lhassa. The two sides of the nave, if it may be so called, are used as a warehouse.

Before we left, the lama who acted as our guide showed us a tambourine which was used as an organ for accompanying the prayers; and striking the cymbals which are used for the same purpose, he, with raised forefinger and open mouth, bade us admire their sonorous properties. Their vibrations are, as a matter of fact, very harmonious. Before parting with him we gave him a handsome "tip," and the poor fellow did not attempt to disguise his satisfaction, for these simple people do not know what wealth is, and we were struck by the wretched state in which the Mongols encamped around the pagoda live. The interior of their tents is the acme of filth, and the smells emanating from them are horrible. Nearly all the children are naked, the parents not having the wherewithal to clothe them. As to the women, they exceed in ugliness anything which can be imagined; and one cannot help wondering how the most ardent of poets would contrive to idealise them.

In the evening we penetrate by a small pass into the valley of the Kunges, and encamp not far from a copper-mine, where we discover a tiny spring, which supplies us with sufficient water for our tea. And that is about all, for we are on an arid steppe.

September 18.—To-day we encamp among the rushes on the banks of the Kunges, at a place named Timurlik. We cross the Kunges about six miles farther on, for we have to make to the south-east towards the valley of Tsakma, and the pass which leads there is higher up the stream. We are now on the route followed by Prjevalsky, and so far the crossing of the chain of the Tien Shan, which barred our route, has presented no great difficulties. The excursion, indeed, was a delightful one, and the temperature agreeable, though at one in the afternoon it was 100° Fahrenheit in the shade. The minimum at night was 16°,

just cool enough to make it a pleasure to wrap ourselves up in
our long wadded blankets.

September 19.—Some Kirghis who to-day offered us hospitality
declared themselves to be the happiest of men. They have water
in plenty; they sow their corn at the foot of the mountains, and
find an abundance of grass in the plains for their flocks and herds.
They do not run short of wood, for the banks of the Kunges are
covered with thick plantations, where the willow, the poplar, the
apple-tree (with small and sharp-flavoured fruit), the pepper-tree,
the apricot-tree, hemp, the liquorice-plant, and the hop-vine grow
wild. These Kirghis formerly lived on Russian territory in the
neighbourhood of Lepsinsk, and crossed over to Chinese soil
because they had no routes for their flocks. They pay the Chinese
a tax of 10 per cent. They are very cheerful, well fed, lusty, and
with plenty of colour, like all who live in the keen mountain air.
They do not strike us as being very fond of work, passing all
their time in going from one tent to another, in eating and sleeping, though occasionally they go out after game. Several of them
are armed with Berdane rifles.

September 20.—We take leave of these Kirghis, the last we
shall see, their tribes not extending farther east. Their chief,
named Sasan, is very proud of the Russian medal which he wears
round his neck, and of the blue button in his hat, which indicates
his Chinese rank. He accompanies us through the reed-beds, and
before wishing us all sorts of good luck, recommends to our
favourable notice five men of his tribe whom we may encounter
in the Yulduz country. He warns us that when they see us they
will take us for Chinese and make off, but he begs us not to fire
on them or do them any harm. We at once inferred that Sasan's
friends are Barantashis—that is to say, persons addicted to *baranta*,
the Turkish word for horse-stealing.

September 22.—The two guides whom the Chinese governor
gave us assert that they do not know the route to the valley of

VALLEY OF THE TSAKMA.

Tsakma, and Abdullah, the interpreter, who undertook to show us the way, led us right into a cul-de-sac. We retraced our steps, and the plainest common sense enabled us to discover what would have been a convenient pass if the rain had not made the ascent so arduous. Gaining the summit at last, we descended into the valley, and re-ascended a plateau, where we found refuge beneath a splendid cluster of pine-trees; a piece of bread taken out of our pockets, and some currants picked from a currant-bush close by, constituting our frugal breakfast.

The rain ceased when we reached the summit of the pass. Near the watershed we came upon a roughly-defined path along the edge of a gorge to our left. All of a sudden a strong gust of wind made a large horizontal rent in the veil of mist spread over the landscape, and we were able to distinguish, far to the south, mountains covered with forests, the trees of which already had a powdering of snow, while above were large banks of black clouds. Then the mist slowly cleared off, and as the atmosphere gradually lightened, the eye wandered gladly over a broad valley, which we did not suspect to be so near. Clumps of green trees mark the windings of the river Tsakma, which traverses a steppe extending towards the west, and covering, as if with a greyish carpet, the sides of the valley. It might be supposed to be perfectly smooth, and to come down without a break to the groves of trees at the bottom; but by looking closer, spots of a more decided colour can be distinguished, and the eye gradually detects that they are moving. They prove to be gazelles, which take fright at our approach, and make off at full speed. It is then we discover that the slope, which had seemed to us quite smooth, is not so in reality, for the gazelles first go down and disappear, then come up again, only again to disappear, disclosing to us all the undulations of a very uneven desert, a few green patches in the hollows marking the places where the water which has come down from the mountain has collected.

The horizon being more distinct, thanks to the breeze, the view broadens towards the west, and stretches so far that the river is only visible as a slender thread, and gradually becomes lost in space. So we get once more that sensation of the desert which we nomads so like. Without attempting to analyse

A MONGOLIAN TENT (*p.* 19).

the feeling, I may say that the steppe, the desert, is a very fascinating place of sojourn for one who has lived in large cities, and has been put out of humour by the petty worries of civilisation. Solitude is a true balm, which heals up the many wounds that the chances of life have inflicted; its monotony has a calming effect upon nerves made over-sensitive from having vibrated too much; its pure air acts as a douche which drives petty ideas out of the head. In the desert, too, the mind sees more clearly, and mental processes are carried on more easily.

Encamping on a natural platform near a plantation through which the river runs, we light big fires, dry our clothes, and sacrifice a good fat sheep. The sheep remaining are fastened together and placed between the fires, within the circle formed by the camels and horses, for we are in fear of the wolves reducing us to starvation.

This region, in which are to be found traces of wild boar, deer, and wolves, is frequented by trappers and hunters, as is proved by the ashes of a fire in the open, by charred logs of wood, and by a shelter made out of the boughs of trees.

We find a very comfortable resting-place under a pine-tree, between two enormous roots. The soil had been trampled down, and our sleeping apartment is a thick bed of grass under a sort of arch, beneath which we have to creep. Of course, it would not do to attempt many gestures in awaking, but one can sleep here protected from nearly all winds, and light a fire without fear of its being put out by the rain, the fine points of the evergreen branches not allowing a drop to penetrate so far. There is an abundance of game close at hand, and we shall clearly be able to kill some stags, since we háve come across big thigh-bones which the wolves have not taken the trouble to crunch. Moreover, there is delicious water and plenty of wood ready to hand.

4

CHAPTER II.

TO KOURLA.

A Good Camping Ground—Tent Life—Arrival of Two Torgots—Death of a Camel—Concerning *Obos*—The Gorge of the Kabchigué-gol—A Native at His Devotions—The Ghadik—Farewell to the Torgots—A Pan-Turkish Empire—Yakoob-Beg.

IMATCH.

September 26.—After a brief stage on the 24th, having found a suitable spot, we halted to prepare for crossing the pass. I may say, once for all, that by " a suitable spot " I mean one where we can pitch our tent upon fairly level ground, sheltered from the wind or the snow, and, if possible, close to wood and water. A splendid camping ground such as this is not to be forgotten, and so we have remained here two days, busied in repairs, examining the horses' shoes and substituting new ones where required, and taking care that there is not a nail loose or missing. The backs of the beasts of burden and of the horses are carefully inspected; where the saddles gall, they are rectified, and the wounds dressed; the saddle-bags and packing canvas are sewn where torn.

Our old camel-driver, the bandy-legged Imatch, who would not part from the camels we had bought of his master, looks after his charges with genuine affection. They know him, and when he calls to them in the steppe at feeding-time, they come to him like fowls to the henwife.

Some of our men are already indisposed, and it happens that these are the most lazy of the whole troop. They are very anxious to be sent back with the guides given us by the governor, who are returning. However, they must go with us beyond the pass, as we cannot afford to reduce our staff just now.

We have been leading a tent-life for barely ten days, and already we have got accustomed to it and have learnt to like it. And yet our tent is neither large nor comfortable. About the height of an average-sized man, it is sufficiently long and broad to enable all three of us to lie upon the felt, to eat out of the single pot around which we gather, and to sip our tea without rubbing elbows. Our shelter consists of a good piece of canvas sewn double, and this suffices to protect us from the bad weather, and to give us the sensation of being in a well-protected room while the rain is pelting and the wind howling outside.

The departure of the two guides provided by the Governor of Ili created a void, which was at once filled up by the arrival of two Torgots. They came in to our encampment on horseback, with their rifles slung across the shoulder, and with a long coil of hair hanging down the back. Approaching our men's fire, they began to converse with them in the Mongolian language, and, after having had some tea, said, in reply to our questions, that five days before they found four of their best horses missing, so they went in search of them. Emerging from the valley of the Yulduz, where their tents were pitched, they found traces of horses, but without knowing whether they were theirs or not. So they resolved to visit the valley of the Tsakma, thinking that the thieves had passed that way. As a matter of fact, they discovered traces northward—that is to say, in the direction of the Kirghis of the Kunges. But, rain falling, they could not trace them any further, so they returned, being certain that they could catch us up, for they saw that we had camels.

Upon our asking them why the Kirghis had stolen their horses, they said it had always been so, and they could not indulge in reprisals, for the Kirghis were the stronger. Formerly they lived in complete security in this valley of the Tsakma. Then the Kirghis came, and at first occupied part of it, but then they wanted to take the whole of it. For some time there was a constant interchange of robberies and murders between the two peoples, until at last the Chinese authorities intervened and decided that the only means of re-establishing peace was to compel the two parties to quit the pastures. "Since that time," they added, "neither Mongols nor Kirghis have lighted their fires in the valley of the Tsakma."

We had no difficulty in inducing the two Torgots to remain with us and show us the way. They were much interested in what went on around them—in the arms which were being furbished, in the birds which were being stuffed, while they were surprised at finding the shin from the leg of a stag which Prince Henry had killed being preserved. They exchanged remarks when they observed the terrible effect produced by the bullet of the express rifle, and then, chin on hand, feasted their eyes upon the palao-meat which was cooking nicely in the pot, the sight of this completing our conquest of them.

September 25.—To-day, after going up hill and down dale, we gradually climb to the pass, which Rachmed and myself consider very easy by comparison with many others. A strong cold wind gets up from the W.N.W.—that is to say, at our back—but we are on a desolate steppe, where we can find neither a shrub nor anything else which can help to combat the cold that is beginning to be unpleasant. On the other hand, we come upon some very pretty flowers, lovely wild pansies and edelweiss that would delight the heart of an Alpinist. In the evening we encamp on the banks of the Yulduz, which we reach by descending a path free from stones. The clouds conceal from us the mountains, which shut in the valley, and this does not add to the attractiveness of the view. We are glad to huddle away in a deep gorge, for the wind is most cutting.

Before night-time all our camels have come in, but one of them, purchased at Kuldja, is ill, and he drops as soon as he has got in. His burden is removed, but he cannot rise. There is a divergency of opinion as to whether he will recover, and the

THE YULDUZ VALLEY.

interpreter, who knows all about everything, says: "Wait a minute, and I will tell you. The hairs of his tail will indicate to you what his fate will be."

He pulls out a few of these hairs and examines them, afterwards pressing them between the thumb and the forefinger, close to the root, and rubbing his two fingers together.

"I can assure you that he will die."

"Why?"

"Because I had no difficulty in pulling out the hairs, because the adipose tissue adheres to the root of the hairs, which indicates a fatal sickness."

The face of the little interpreter glows with satisfaction at having given proof of his sagacity; and in the meanwhile our poor camel is in his death throes, exciting the pity of his driver, who puts a sheepskin under his head for a pillow. The dying beast's eye is dilated and he loses consciousness. He struggles as he lies, and one would fancy that all the thoughts of his past existence were chasing one another hurriedly through his brain. He seems as if anxious to go through all the acts which have been so often reiterated as to have become habits with him. He makes an effort to rise, he kicks his legs in the air as if to walk, he moves his jaws as if to eat, he seeks to make a noise in the throat as if to ruminate; but the gaze fades away, the eye closes, and the good servant gasps in death.

The two Torgots, who are Buddhists, look on with much sadness, and mumble some kind of a prayer—or, rather, a few words wishing a safe journey to the soul which is on the point of transmigration. That does not prevent them, as soon as the soul has taken its flight, from stripping the skin off the body which held it. As the soul has fled, what could it matter?

September 26.—To-night we have a minimum of four degrees below zero, and when they wake up the men complain of the cold. We follow the valley, which continues to run through the steppe, and, gradually getting farther away from the Yulduz, the waters of which flow over sand and pebbles, we encamp on the banks of the Zakiste-gol, a river abounding in fish. On the way, we meet the caravan of an important lama, and make him very uneasy by proceeding to photograph him, Prince Henry succeeding none the less. These worthy lamas, with their pointed head-gear, seem to us to be a little the worse for drink.

The landscape remains much the same; for we are still on the steppe shut in by mountains, bare, and in places quite white with salt, while here and there are peat-pits, where the water is either stagnant or runs off very slowly. We notice some *arkar* horns on the ground, but have no time to go in pursuit of these animals on the mountain.

September 28.—This evening we encamp beyond the dried-up bed of the river Borokusté, and find plenty of grass for the camels and *kisiak* (droppings) for the fire. To the north we can see on the sides of the mountain an inscription in very large letters. These are the sacred sayings of the Buddhists, which believers can decipher miles off. Never in my life have I seen such big letters; all the slopes of the Tien Shan would scarcely be sufficient to print a whole book. The Buddhists like to manifest their devotion in the open air, and when we leave the valley to reach by a pass the defile of Kabchigué-gol, we meet *obos,* or heaps of stones, upon most of which prayers have been engraved,.at each culminating point of the undulating ground.

These *obos* are generally placed on an eminence, at one of those spots where the beasts of burden are allowed to halt and get breath. Advantage is often taken of these halts to make a light collation; after that, prayers are offered that the road may be a good one, when starting on a journey, while thanks are returned because it has been good, if the journey is ending. By way of showing respect or gratitude to the divinity, stones are heaped up, and a pole is often placed in the ground, with a prayer written on a piece of canvas tied to the end of it; those who follow after add more stones. Workmen specially employed, and travelling lamas, engrave prayers upon slabs and deposit them at the spot. Thus the *obo* is constituted, and the shepherds, the travellers, and the tribes on the march swell its proportions every time they pass, the heaps of stones gradually acquiring such colossal proportions that they have the appearance of monuments. Many Buddhists deposit images of Buddha, and of Tsong Kaba, the great reformer; and small pyramids of earth represent chapels, as I was informed. Others deposit carved fragments of horn, pieces torn off their garments, bits of horsehair (which they tie on to a stick), or anything which comes handy to them; and when they are making the presentation, they offer up prayer.

In order to reach the defile of Kabchigué-gol—a word which, we are told, means "river of the narrow place"—we follow the left side of the valley. The road, which is fairly good, winds along the spurs of the mountain, with a view to the right of the valley where the Torgots have their tents, with their flocks and herds roaming over the green steppe. The sun is shining in all its splendour, and its heat seems excessive after the severe cold of the previous night. We have only to look behind us to be convinced that this fine weather will not last, for we can see the dark mass of a storm coming upon us from the extremity of the valley. The wind howls, the sleet and then the snow beat down upon us with all the severity of winter. Fortunately we have reached the summit of the pass—those of us, at least, who have horses, for the camels come at a slower rate, and do not alter their pace.

The fury of the storm is intensified at the very moment I reach the large *obo* which indicates the beginning of the descent. I am alone, and the opportunity for helping myself to some of the numerous stones with prayers engraved upon them is too good to be resisted. But I had reckoned without the spirit of the mountain, who makes my horse so restive that he will not move a step forward. I determine to dismount and tie him up somewhere, but there is nothing to be found which would answer the purpose; so I get up again, and once more endeavour to bring him up to the *obo*, but the noise of the stones striking against one another in the wind frightens him again, and, after losing my astrachan cap, I have to give up the attempt in despair. All these incidents did not prevent us from meeting in the evening beneath the willows of Kabchigué-gol.

IMATCH CALLING THE CAMELS.

5

October 2.—We have remained at this spot for three days, partridges swarming and enabling the guns of our party to make large bags; they are grey in colour and very succulent. Thrushes, tomtits, and wagtails throng the brushwood and trees growing on the mountain-side. We are in the country of the Torgots, and the two who have accompanied us have their tent in this pass. They are not rich, but own a few head of stock—horses, cows, and sheep. They are the descendants of the Kalmucks who left the steppes of the Volga in 1779, and found their way back after much hardship to the land of Ili. Those nomads that we meet have preserved a vague tradition of this great exodus, and they tell us that they came from the country of the Orosses (Russians), "where we left the people of our race. It is about 200 years that we have inhabited the Tien Shan." But they can give us no details; they have forgotten the sufferings and the energy of their ancestors. They show us their square caps with flaps for the ears in sheepskin, and they assert that this form of headdress comes to them from the Russians. This shows how difficult it is to get authentic information as to the history of Asia.

We were not sorry to leave this narrow gorge of the Kabchigué-gol, despite its wildness and picturesqueness, and its wonderful spring, which cures rheumatism, and which is called Archan Buluk, that is to say, "the spring of healing." We meet a few patients here, Mongolians of small stature, well built, with very small hands and feet—not the broad hands of the toiler, but the elongated hands of the unoccupied. Their head is very much like a ball which has scarcely had the corners squared off, their cheek-bones are prominent, their eyes are imperceptible, and, when seen in profile, it is scarcely possible to distinguish the nose. A lama owns a small hut near the spring, under an elm-tree, and he is at once the consulting physician and the manager of this primitive bathing establishment. From him we learned

AN "OBO."

that the young Khan, who is the heir of the Torgots, has started on a pilgrimage for Thibet.

Making a start, we emerged from the defile on to the steppe, the approach to which was heralded three-quarters of a mile in advance by bunches of *yantag*, upon which the camels fed with manifest delight. The change is a very abrupt one, for all of a sudden we are amid stones and sand, with a vast horizon; the temperature has already risen, and while an hour ago the air was fresh and pleasant, we now begin to sweat. Marching along beside a narrow channel for irrigation, we reached a surface dotted with reed-beds, where the Torgots were busy upon the wheat harvest, and encamped upon fallow ground, close to a fine elm with an *obo* beside it. Under the shade of the tree is a sort of altar, analogous to the *ara* of the Romans, in the hollow part of which we can see ashes and charcoal, odoriferous plants being burnt upon it in honour of the divinity. Resting against the trunk of the tree is a whole bundle of sticks with rags and slabs of wood, with prayers written on them, while in the branches are a number of skins of lambs and goats, in an advanced state of decomposition, which have been hung there as votive offerings. Towards evening, at the hour when one is inclined to reverie, my attention is excited by a murmur which seems to be drawing nearer and nearer in the tall grass. A man appears, well advanced in years, the shoulders bent, and a chaplet in his hand. He casts an uneasy glance at me, but without breaking off his murmuring, and, standing upright before the *obo*, he tells his beads; then, going up to the tree, stoops down and rubs his forehead with the sap which he has let run on to his fingers from the bark. He next picks up two or three leaves, presses them in his hand, and, having again looked at us, makes off without saying a word, muttering as he goes, " Om mané padmé houm "—a phrase which thousands of men repeat all their lives without understanding its meaning, but believing that they are ensuring for

SANDHILLS AT KOURLA.

themselves a happy future.   In the course of the day Prince Henry
had great difficulty in photographing some of the Torgots who
were prowling about our bivouac.   Only one of them would accept
the money we offered him as a consideration for giving a sitting.
They do not understand the box which is turned upon them, and
they generally make off at the sight of it with terror depicted on
their countenance.   Like children, savages are always afraid of
what they do not understand; and if the person photographed
should happen to fall ill in the course of the year, his illness
would be attributed to "that box the Europeans had with them."
We observe that the young men in some cases wear a sort of silver
ornament in the left ear, and we are told that this is an engagement to marry the girl who has received the fellow-earring
as a present.

October 3.—We are again on the steppe, where we see the
thorny plant which the nomads call *touia kuiruk* (camel's tail) and
the sweet *yantag,* on which our camels feed with delight whenever
they get the chance.   Then the approach to the river Ghadik,
whose waters fall into the lake of Karashar, is announced by tents,
*saklis,** and cultivated fields.   The Ghadik, as it runs down
from the Tien Shan, ramifies over a considerable surface, as if
delighted to be at liberty in the open plain ; and it embraces a
great number of islands which are almost buried beneath a vegetation quickened by periodical inundations.   We encamped in the
tall grass of one of these islands, our tent being shut in by a thick
grove of willows, elms, tamarisks, jujube and liquorice trees.
There is no trace of any paths upon this archipelago, for they
have been effaced by the waters, and we requisitioned some
Torgots to guide us through the grassy labyrinth.

We emerged from it in about two hours, after having crossed

---

* The name of *sakli* is given to the walled square within which the tents and the
flocks are enclosed during the winter. In most cases some sort of a shelter or hut is
built in one corner, which serves as a shed or cooking-place when the cold is very
severe.

several arms of the river, which are very deep at flood-time, and which are certainly not fordable then. In fact, we are told that when the snows melt, the Ghadik forms a regular lake, with the tops of the trees just above the water. The pasturage is excellent, and constitutes the wealth of the tribes grouped around the king of the Torgots.

We had no sooner crossed the last irrigating canal which derives its waters from the Ghadik than the desert began. The transition is a very sudden one, and there is a difference of temperature before we have gone a hundred yards. Behind us the air is moist and comparatively warm, but here it is dry and very keen. A path, which has been trodden in by camels at a time when the soil was softened by rain, winds its way upwards to a deeper depression, running in a S.S.E. direction, in a small mountain chain very abrupt and bare.

Beyond, there is a sort of valley without water, sandy, and skirted by elevations of the soil, which are full of deep furrows and seem crumbling away, with the appearance of some abandoned city whose monuments are falling to ruins.

Further on, in the land of the black-tree (*Kara motoun*), a name given to a species of elm planted along the irrigating watercourses, we again encounter the Torgots. The last of the Mongolian Torgots are to be found here; they cultivate a few plots of the land which is not very fertile, since it is mixed with salt.

A number of tall, well-set-up men, with black bushy beards, come round our bivouac; we have not seen such men since leaving Siberia and Kuldja. They enter into conversation with our men in Turkish, greeting them in the Mahometan fashion, and one of them at once makes off, and speedily returns with some melons which recall those of Turkestan by their oblong shape and delicious taste. We all of us—French, Russians, Tarantshis, Kirghis, and Uzbegs—are pleased at this meeting with men whom we feel to be closer to us than the Mongols. We feel as if we had met some old acquaintances, and a very merry evening is passed.

If the principle of nationalities—determined by unity of language—ever prevails among those who speak Turkish, if a kingdom be reconstituted out of the scattered members of this great nation, the monarch or the caliph of it will never see the sun set upon his dominions, and will command a countless host of valiant warriors. But they would be scattered over more than three-fourths of the surface of the Old World, and this would render it difficult to mobilise them in the event of war.

October 5.—To-day we have entered upon the last stage which separates us from Kourla. We again traversed a corner of the desert, and, as yesterday, low chains of crumbling marl, also having the aspect of turrets, cupolas, and mausoleums. Before getting near to the Kontshé-Darya, on a height commanding a full view of the plain, we could distinguish the remains of a fort of dry brick built by Yakoob the " blessed one," also surnamed " the dancer " by the people of the Ferghana.

This man was made in the mould to do great things, and Prjevalsky was struck with his intelligence when he had an interview with him at Kourla in 1877. The good fortune of Yakoob was prodigious, though his rise was slow, for he was a man of mature age when he became master of Kashgar and Chinese Turkestan. During the few years that he governed this country he displayed no ordinary activity, covering it with useful buildings, tracing canals, and organising an army after the European model, having recruited, through the medium of the Sultan, officers in all countries of Europe. Several came from Turkey, and a member of the present French Chamber of Deputies was on the point of being employed by Yakoob. Heaven only knows what would have happened if this hardy Uzbeg had not been checked in his career. He would certainly have got together the " twelve thousand good soldiers "

whom Lord Hastings in his day considered sufficient for the conquest of China (this was Prjevalsky's estimate also of what would
be required), and we should have witnessed the constitution of a
Turco-Mongolian State, which would have extended from the
Terek-Davan, at the north of the Pamir, to the gulf of Petchili.
But Allah had decided that Yakoob was not to go beyond
Kourla, and it was there that he closed his interesting career, in
the fortress built by him, which still exists. He died of poison,
administered by his Prime Minister, to whom the Chinese made
alluring promises, which they took good care not to keep.

In Yakoob's lifetime the people were dissatisfied at having
been aroused out of the state of torpor so agreeable to the people
of Asia. Now this same people, which is under the administration of the Chinese, regrets the " good time " of the *Badoulet*
(the " blessed one"), who is spoken of as having been a great
man, while the *bakshi* sing his great deeds at the festivals. They
are so anxious for a fresh master that they ask us, hailing
as we do from the West, if "the Russians are soon coming to
take us ? "

A MONGOLIAN LAMA.

CHAPTER III.

FROM KOURLA TO TCHARKALIK.

Kourla—In the Bazaar—Provisioning the Caravan—Parpa—Visit from the *Akim* of Kourla: A "Mandarinade"—Tchinagi—Music in the Camp—A Forest of Poplars—Crossing the Kontché-Darya and the Intchigué-Darya—Aktarma—The River Tarim—The "Silk Plant"—Arkan—Hard Words and Blows Compared—Talkitchin—The Last of the Tarim—At Tcharkalik.

KOURLA WOMEN.

October 6.—Kourla is a small town situated in a fine oasis. It is traversed by the Kontché-Darya, over which a wooden bridge has been built, connecting the suburbs on the left bank with the bazaars and the fortress on the right. The population is a mixture of Chinese, Dungans, and Tarantshis; but, as the Mussulmans form the majority, the chief of the town (the *Akim*) is of that persuasion. It was he who came and laid siege to us upon our arrival, not giving us time to enjoy the satisfactions and pleasures which an oasis always offers to those who have crossed the desert. And Kourla is charming, with its gardens, its green trees, its fine river, and its bazaars, where are to be found melons, apples, figs, grapes, and apricots, which nomads like ourselves find so delicious.

We arrived last night, having done a stage of nearly thirty-five miles. We are lodged in the house of a Mussulman, who is a Russian subject and a merchant in the town.

To-day we received a great many inquisitive visitors. We learn that the authorities are summoned to meet at the *yamen* in the evening to take counsel together concerning us, and the chief asks permission to pay us a visit to-morrow morning.

We find ourselves in the first bazaar we have seen since we left Kuldja, and we shall not encounter another after we make a fresh start. So we buy and buy in preparation for Thibet, and, without losing an hour, hire twenty-two camels to carry our purchases. Among these purchases are 1,600 Russian pounds of bread, done down in fat and salt, made up into small cakes about as thick as the finger and as broad as the palm of a man's hand. The reason of their being made so small is that a biscuit of this size is easy to stow away; it can, if necessary, be placed up the sleeve on the march, for it may happen that while one is munching it one may have to pick up one's gun or whip. Moreover, it represents in size almost exactly what the appetite at such a time demands, and not an atom is lost. The salt aids the digestion, and the fat is, of course, a preventive against cold. The purchases also include 520 pounds of the best flour, which will be kept in reserve, for we shall only use these provisions at the last extremity; 280 pounds of mutton, salted and done up in skins; 160 pounds of small raisins, very delicate in flavour, with no pips, called "kishmish," which will be mixed with rice, and only distributed later, when the cold, the salt meat, the forced marches, and the great altitude have brought about that state of weakness which is so like scurvy; 80 pounds of salt, though we are pretty safe to find plenty in the desert, on the surface of the soil, or on the shores of the lakes; 80 pounds of sesamum oil for hasty puddings; tobacco, bags, pieces of felt, and 6,000 pounds of barley for our horses, although the interpreter Abdullah, and a man named Parpa, an inhabitant of Kourla, tell us that we need not concern ourselves about them.

The man Parpa was formerly in the service of Carey and Dalgleish, the English travellers, and we have engaged him in the hope that he will furnish us with useful information. This adventurer, with a long black beard, very taciturn, and with a tragic air, is a native of the Ferghana, who came with Yakoob-Beg into

A BIT OF THE TARIM.

Chinese Turkestan. He gets the horses shod, makes saddles for the camels, and has the reputation of being a brave man.

The preparations are rapidly completed; we have treated with a Dungan whom we are to pay a high price, but he will bring with him three servants, two Dungans, and a Turkish Mussulman from the oasis of Hami.

October 7.—Returning to the house to-day, we find the servants of the *Akim*, who announce the coming of their master. Soon afterwards there arrive, followed by an escort, some mandarins, dressed in the Mahometan style, but with the Chinese headdress, a globular hat, and wearing the pigtail which is the mark of vassaldom that the Chinese exact from the Mahometans, whose head is generally shaved. These head men of the town, most of them advanced in years, enter our room. We offer them

INHABITANTS OF KOURLA.

seats on the white felt which has been unrolled for them, and wait for them to question us, without uttering a word. They begin the conversation in Chinese, politely asking as to our health, congratulating us upon having made a safe journey, and promising

us their help. Between whiles their attendants place before
us an offering of dried fruits, melons, and almonds, in accordance
with the custom of Turkestan. We thank them with the
utmost cordiality for their good nature, and wait to see what is
to follow. It is easy to see that the chiefs are somewhat em-
barrassed; they exchange a few words, and then the one who is
highest in rank begins to make a rather solemn speech, pointing out that it is a habit to ask strangers for their papers. To
which I reply that it is a very good custom, as it is impossible to
take too many precautions with regard to strangers who come on
to the territory of others. As concerns ourselves, he has seen by
our cards on red paper, and written in Chinese characters, that
one of us is a prince allied to the Kings of the West, and he
must be aware the White Pasha has facilitated our passage
through his States; and we hope the Emperor of China will
not be less obliging. Although we did not understand why
papers should be demanded of us at Kourla, after we had been
allowed to cross the frontier and go through the province of Ili,
we were willing, in order to please him, as he was so kind to us,
to let him have the general pass, which had been seen by the
Governor of the province of Ili. He asked our leave to keep it,
which we gave all the more readily because we know from
Prjevalsky and others that in China papers are only of service
at places where they are not required. After an interchange of
respectful and dignified greetings the chiefs went off.

What will happen to-morrow? We foresee complications, and
Rachmed, who is much affected by all this, fully realises our
position. He says, "It is the beginning of the 'old story'; the
Chinese are going to bother us as much as they can. It is not
surprising on the part of people who eat pork." And so Rachmed
rattles on, loading with opprobrium this people, which allows its
women to have wooden legs, which emits an odour intolerable to
a true Mussulman, and so on.

The chief result of this interview is to make us hurry forward our preparations, for we have seen the advance-guard to-day; the declaration of war will be brought to us to-morrow.

The same evening before sunset the chiefs of Kourla arrive in full dress, and, almost before the greetings have been exchanged and the cups of tea served, the *Akim* tells us to visit the Governor of Karashar before continuing our journey. We reply that the Governor is a person of too little consequence for us to turn aside from our route to go and see him. "If he wishes to say anything to us, let him come and say it. Moreover, he must have seen our papers."

"Your papers are of no value, and, to tell you the truth, here is the order to arrest you which has arrived at Karashar from Ouroumitchi."

We display great surprise at this, and ask him to let one of our men read the order. And then the conversation is resumed as follows:

"Where is our pass then?"

"At Karashar."

"Well, we shall keep your order until you have restored the paper we confided to you, for you have it in your possession, and you are not speaking the truth."

I accordingly take the order, put it into my pocket, and request them to go.

The small Chinese mandarin who had brought it gets as pale as his yellow complexion permits, and begs us to restore it, making a motion with his hand across his throat as much as to say that he will lose his head if he does not get the order back. I repeat that he shall have it if they restore us our pass, and when they again deny having it we make them leave, saying that the sun has set, and we want to rest.

They go off crestfallen, and a few minutes later one of the chiefs returns, holding the pass in his hand. He offers it to us and we take it back, promising to restore him his order, but not till the next day, in order that we may have it photographed.

A CHINESE WARRANT.

This photograph is reproduced above, and the translation has been made by the Marquis d'Hervey de St. Denys. It is as follows:—

"I, Han, sub-prefect, having the honorary title of Fou-tchi, fulfilling the duties of prefect of the district of Kola-Chacul (Karashar), have received from the temporary governor Wei an order thus conceived: 'At the present time, a prince of the

blood in the kingdom of France, Ken-li-ho (Henry), travelling
without a Chinese passport and on his own initiative, is making
toward Lo-pou-ta-cul (Lob Nor). I order the local authorities,
in no matter what place the French prince may be found, to
prevent him from continuing his route and to turn him back.'
In consequence of this order my duty is to send out agents to
gather information, and I accordingly direct two agents to
proceed at once to Kou-cul-li (Kourla), and to act in concert
with the Mussulman chiefs of this locality in order to inspect
the country. If the French prince is met, his progress must be
arrested, and he must be prevented from penetrating any farther
and compelled to turn back. The agents must not be guilty of
negligence or delay under pain of incurring penalties. This
must not be disobeyed. Twice recommended, and his instructions
are given to Tchang-Youy, and to A-li. They will take care to
conform to them. The eighth day of the ninth moon of the
fifteenth year of Kouang-Sin. Valid until the return, to be
afterwards given back and annulled."

I might, with reference to this order, say a good deal as to
the perfidy of the Chinese with regard to Europeans of all kinds,
even to Europeans who have behaved generously towards mandarins. But it would be a waste of space, for in the course of
this narrative the reader will have opportunities of appreciating
at its proper value the administration of provinces remote from
the frontier and the coast. On the northern frontier, one
encounters, side by side with the mandarins, Russian consuls who
command not only respect but obedience, while on the coast there
are consuls and persons of all nationalities who maintain amicable
relations with the mandarins. But in the interior of the empire
the situation is not the same.

October 8.—The chiefs of Kourla, with the Akim at their head,
return to see us again, and we restore to them the order. They repeat that we cannot continue our route. We reply that nothing

7

will stop us from going to the Lob Nor, where we wish to enjoy the chase. When we are ready, we shall load our beasts and start, and if any effort is made to stop us by force there will be bloodshed, and the blood will be upon their heads. We are not evil-doers; we do no harm to anyone, and why should we not enjoy the immunities accorded to the smallest of traders? We tell the *Akim* that this is our ultimatum, and bid him reflect. He hangs his head down, and, dropping the Chinese language in his emotion, says in his native Turkish:—" I am only executing the orders given me. I do not wish you any harm. I can see you are not bad people. What would you have me do? I am in a cruel position, for my life is at stake. Truly, I am like the nut between two stones; by Allah, I am!"

And he heaves a sigh which does not seem to be affected.

" Help me," he went on to say. " I will go to Karashar and see my superior. Let one of your party come with me; he will explain things, and, by the help of Allah, matters will all be arranged."

" It is impossible to do as you ask, *Akim*," I reply, " for the explanations are already given. We do not in any way recognise your sub-prefect; and the step would be quite useless, for if one of us were to go to Karashar and your superior persisted in stopping us, we should start just the same."

The chief and his companions then rose and took leave of us.

October 9.—A fresh visit from the *Akim*, who insists, with a pretty firm air, upon our retracing our steps. Upon our categorically refusing, he gets up, without pressing the matter any further, and says that he shall have to resort to force—a threat which makes us laugh.

The *Aksakal* of the Russian subjects in Kourla then intervenes, and tells us that he has been threatened with having a chain put round his neck and being dragged off to Karashar if he lends us assistance. A strong force arrives from Karashar to reinforce the feeble garrison of Kourla, which consisted of sixty soldiers, who seem to us more or less stupefied with opium.

We hurry on our preparations for starting. The purchases are completed, the saddles for the camels are sewn, and there is nothing to delay us any longer. At nightfall a delegation of chiefs, comprising the *Aksakal*, come and make a formal remonstrance with us, but at last they see that we are firmly resolved not to let ourselves be stopped.

After supper we let the men sleep until midnight, and then wake them up and give them orders to get all the loads ready, and not to utter a word. All the preliminaries of the start are soon got through. A few hours later I get up without making the slightest noise, and satisfy myself that for the nonce the soundest sleepers have sharp ears.

October 10.—At daylight all our camels and horses are ready, well shod and well saddled. The news of our starting soon spreads through the town, and the caravan is organised in the presence of a multitude which invades our courtyard, and which we are obliged to drive out with a good stout stick. Some pickpockets have managed to sneak up to our things and steal whatever they can conceal about their persons. We prevent the recurrence of this by creating a void about us. Our attitude is, at the same time, a warning to the mandarins that we are prepared for any eventuality, as yesterday.

Having been sent to the bazaar to procure a few delicacies, our Chinaman returns and says that the merchants are of opinion that the *Akim* has arranged the matter very well, since he has induced us to write to Karashar. I forgot to mention yesterday that we had promised to send a few lines of explanation to the sub-prefect of Karashar. In this letter, which was translated into Turkish and Chinese, we stated our intention of going to shoot in the neighbourhood of the Lob Nor, where we should remain long enough for all the necessary papers to arrive from Pekin or elsewhere. The *Akim's* friends consider that he has managed matters very adroitly, that he has gained a diplomatic victory; in short, to use the language of the country, that "he has had the wit to preserve the face and to add a plume to his hat."

The loading of the beasts of burden is completed, the presents have been distributed to our hosts and acquaintances, the men leap into the saddle and raise their hands to their beards, exclaiming, "Allah is great!" And so *en route* for the Lob Nor.

Two of our men who are riding the best horses go on in front. They are told not to lose sight of the leading camel-driver, and I can see them both. In case of an alarm they are to gallop back to us. When we get close to the gate, Rachmed will go on ahead of all the rest, to see for himself. Now the caravan gets into motion, and proceeds slowly along the street; the camels pack as close to one another as they can, and, swinging their necks and rolling from side to side, they methodically stretch out their long legs, quite indifferent to the teasing of the Chinese, but feeling perhaps the warmth of the superb autumn sun.

On such a delightful day I feel that nothing unpleasant can occur to us; Nature is too bright and smiling for that. While the camels are chewing the cud after their meal of the sweet morning grass, I am ruminating on what remains to be done, and rejoicing inwardly at having begun the second stage of our journey, which will terminate at the Lob Nor. While watching the idlers posted on the roofs, and the women with unveiled faces who are peeping through the half-open doors, replying at the same time by a salaam to the salaam of a boy with a merry and good-humoured face, and by a brandishing of my whip to another not so well-behaved, I am reminded of similar starts from similar countries, and my imagination travels at a bound to Turkestan, Bokhara, and Khiva. I note here the same faces, the same gestures, the same attitudes as there. I can distinguish the

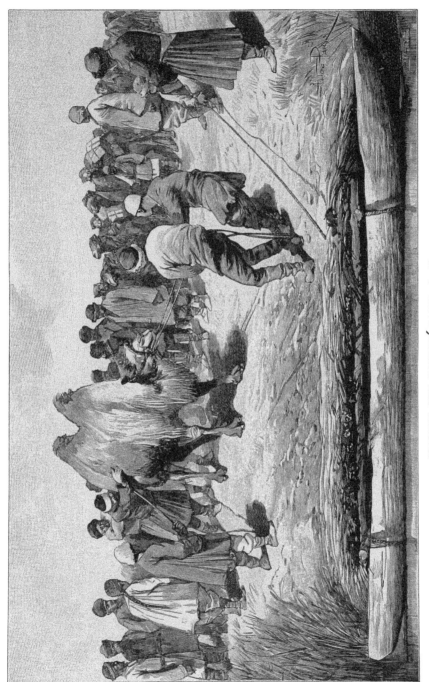

CROSSING THE KONTCHÉ-DARYA (p. 60).

same odours emitted from the houses, and the vast firmament over our heads is of the same inimitable blue, which even the turquoise cannot reproduce. It seems impossible that our journey should be rudely interrupted, commenced as it is in such bright sunshine; the earth presents itself under too smiling an aspect to deceive us afterwards.

For a little way we skirted the crenellated walls of the town, against which are built various earthen huts with creepers growing up them, and then we said good-bye to Kourla and made southward. The road which leads out of the oasis is dusty, and branches out into paths which get lost in the desert, as rivulets exhaust a river before it has reached the end of its course.

On arriving at the last of the *saklis*, we bought some sheep from a friend of the *Aksakal* of the Russian subjects. Although we are certain of having enough to feed men and beasts as far as the Lob Nor, it is as well to have with one a small flock of fat sheep, as a matter of precaution; this, again, will enable us to purchase others of the natives at a lower figure for our daily consumption, for when they see that we are not at their mercy, they will not put up their prices.

October 11.—We had loaded some of our camels when we saw the dust rising on the plain in the direction of Kourla, and presently recognised the chiefs of Kourla in full dress, accompanied by several horsemen. When they got close to our bivouac, they politely dismounted, and one of their attendants came to ask for an audience on the part of his masters. This we at once granted, and the chiefs advanced with a certain degree of haste, no doubt to signify thereby that they were under the influence of some strong emotion. They had smiling faces, they shook hands cordially with us, and leaned forward as they did so, their whole attitude being one of sympathy. They had no sooner seated themselves on the white felt which had been

laid down in their honour, the younger ones remaining on their
feet out of deference, than they hastened to tell us that they had

NATIVES OF YANGI KOUL (*p.* 65).

come as friends, and that they wished us a safe journey and good
health.　They had been compelled to execute the orders sent from

Karashar, but had done so much against their own inclina-
tions. They could see very clearly that we were great personages
and honest people. One of them invited us to believe that the
Akim was a very good fellow; another whispered into the ear of
one of our men that we should do well to mark our gratitude and
forgiveness by a few little presents, such as our hosts at Kourla
had received the day before.

We thanked them politely and gave orders for presents to be
handed to the chiefs as souvenirs of our visit, and at the same
time asked for a guide to introduce us to the people we should
meet on the way, and who would facilitate the passage of the
Kontché-Darya, a river which has no bridges or ferries, and which
has to be crossed on a raft.

We were at once furnished with a man of about sixty, named
Ata Rachmed, the same who formerly accompanied Prjevalsky in
his excursion to the Lob Nor. Our interpreter, Abdullah, recognised him and assured us that Rachmed was the best of men.
Formerly attached to the person of Yakoob, he passed into the
service of the *Akim* of Kourla.

After having received our small gifts, the chiefs rose to their
feet, wished us a safe journey once more, and pressed our hands
very effusively; they then mounted their horses and cantered back
towards Kourla, while we packed up our things, and regained
our cavavan, which was making its way towards the like village
of Tchinagi.

Such is the end of what I must style a "mandarinade," for
this is the only name to give to the series of worries to which
the Chinese mandarins treat Europeans in order to prove to them
that China possesses an "administration." I have related this
incident too much in detail, perhaps; but I believe that I shall
have done a service to future travellers by showing that it is not
well to be alarmed at the threats of the mandarins, and that one
may travel pretty comfortably in this region of the Chinese

8

Empire, always provided that one keeps clear of the large cities, where a countless population does not scruple to commit acts of cowardice and ferocity with the certainty of escaping punishment.

After nine or ten miles of the desert, we bivouacked near the village of Tchinagi, on the banks of a canal planted with willows.

At Tchinagi the aged Ata Rachmed got together a score of woebegone men, whom we promised to pay well if they would help us to construct our rafts on the Kontché-Darya. Among the number was one who had the broad face of the Kirghis, the same small eyes, scanty beard, and guttural way of speaking. On being questioned, he told us that he was a native of the neighbour-hood of Semipalatinsk, and that, having come into the country in Yakoob-Beg's time, with one of his brothers, he had married there and settled in it. "That's like me," exclaimed our Russian, Borodjin; "I served at Kuldja and then at Djarkent, where I married, and I never returned home to Tobolsk." I note this trifling incident in order to point out that on many occasions I have observed that Russians and Turks move from place to place very readily, and especially that they soon abandon all idea of returning to their native country, even when they have left it more or less under compulsion. To inhabitants of the vast and monotonous plain, with horizons as boundless as those of the sea, it matters little at what point of the ocean—for such the plain really is—they may live; they want only a few birch-trees, lighting up the landscape with their silver trunks, a river full of fish, the banks of which, covered with reeds, give shelter to water-fowl and wild boars, and with that a few patches of cultivated ground around the small wooden or earthen hut.

The inhabitants of Tchinagi, who resemble the Sarthians of Turkestan, say that they came from Andidjan—that is to say, from Ferghana—about a hundred years ago. This does not mean anything definite, for Eastern people, as I have said, are incredibly negligent as to dates.

An old man talked to us of Russians whom he had seen in the country, and we know, as a matter of fact, that some of the Old Believers came as far as the Lob Nor in search of land a long time ago. Then we listened to some singers who played upon a two-stringed guitar, and, as we were free in distributing tea and rice, a good part of the village surrounded us, our men dancing to the sound of the accordion, after the custom of their country, and the evening passing in festivity. Even our old camel-driver, carried away by the music, executed a rude sort of a dance with his feeble legs, the Chinaman being the only one who did not stir. Upon our asking him to give us a specimen of the dancing in his district, he replied :—

"Oh, we don't dance; we amuse ourselves by sitting down and doing nothing."

"And what is your music like ? "

"Oh! our music is very similar to that which you hear." And he endeavours to prove this by singing an air, but the effort is so unmusical, despite his extreme seriousness, that we cannot help laughing outright. It does not take much to amuse travellers.

After having crossed a strip of desert, we soon reach a regular forest of poplars. But they are not the same trees as the French poplars; for these grow on the sand, the bark is all wrinkled, and the hollow trunks are covered all over with bindweed. Their foliage varies very much, for the leaves are oblong in the lower branches, and resemble those of the willow, while above they are like those of the ordinary poplar. It is with these trees that we shall have to construct our rafts, and this will increase the difficulty not a little, for this *Populus diversifolia* is porous and dry internally, although its bark is extremely hard, while if it remains long in the water it sinks to the bottom.

On the advice of an old man, who directs the work, and who swears by his white beard, three rows of beams are placed one upon the other; they are tied together and flanked by thick bundles of reeds, so as to elevate the floating line. The raft will only be put into the water at the last moment. In this conjuncture our Russians, accustomed to the water, like all their fellow-countrymen, are very useful to us. As to Rachmed, who has nearly been drowned on several occasions, and who has a horror of all kinds of navigation, he bemoans his fate, and implores, with a very comical face, to be allowed to retrace his steps, for he is sure he shall be drowned.

October 12.—The evening is spent in getting together the trees which have been cut in the forest, or which have been hidden away on the river-banks. They have already been used for making rafts, and the natives drag them to our camp with oxen.

October 13.—The smaller baggage is loaded in canoes, and a sort of ferry is organised by means of rafts. The raft is covered with earth to place our camels under the illusion that they are on *terra firma*. They are not at all fond of the water, and it is even necessary, in order to get them on to the raft, to prepare a sort of landing-stage with stakes and faggots, for the bank is steep. At the first attempt we succeed in getting two camels on to the raft; we keep their heads down by pulling at the ring placed in their noses. The raft is pulled across by a rope, and when the passengers have been landed, it is brought back to the landing-stage by means of another rope. But this time there is the greatest difficulty in getting a camel to advance; persuasion, ruse, and blows are alike powerless, and at last the beast has to be carried. But it slips backwards, its hind legs dropping into the water, while the rest of its body remains on the raft, and in this posture it is pulled across, like a schoolboy lolling over his desk. So we go on until they have all been got over, the horses as well as the sheep swimming across.

This operation lasts all day, and the work is accomplished in very good humour, the Mussulmans sandwiching between it the prayers to which they are called by their mollah.

The natives again speak to us of Yakoob-Beg, and it is clear they regret him very much. They would like to be

CANOE ON THE TARIM.

delivered from the Chinese, who, they say, "eat dogs, and even children."

By nightfall the crossing of the Kontché-Darya is completed, and we distribute numerous "tips" to the workmen who have been employed, leaving them also a couple of sheep.

As the Huns and the Tartars mostly had horses, they were able to cross the rivers and streams pretty easily. The armies which possessed elephants could soon construct rafts, as these animals could drag trees along with their trunks, and probably hauled the baggage, and even people, as almost certainly happened with Hannibal in crossing the Rhone. The camel of Central

Asia is made for a desert without water, and he only likes rivers that he may drink greedily of them.

We make for the Lob Nor by the itinerary which Prjevalsky and Carey followed. At times, however, we are obliged to diverge from it, as inundations have modified the aspect of the country, and we prefer making a détour if we can thereby avoid constructing a raft.

October 14.—Our route lies through the *tougrak* woods, which give a little variety to the violet tamarisk-trees. These *tougraks*, or poplars, are burnt in many places. Flocks of sheep have been roaming through the woods, and traces of them are visible upon the saline soil, into which the foot sinks as into ashes covered over with a light crust. The trees are less thick on the sand-hills, for in this region a great many people come and go. In the afternoon we cross the Intchigué-Darya, a small river which forms another arm of the Tarim, but the crossing is effected by a bridge, which is repaired to admit of the camels going over it. In the evening we encamp at Goumbas, near a piece of water on a bare hill. The natives bring us some trout, and are very well satisfied with the pieces of money which we give them. For our bivouac we prefer a clearing where the breeze will rid us of the mosquitoes, which bite us to death, even under our coverings. There is an abundance of waterfowl, wild geese, ducks, teal, and cormorants in the reed-beds. This region is very sparsely inhabited.

October 15.—To-day we start for Aktarma, which is noted on Prjevalsky's map. It is always the same sandy desert, which reminds some of us of the Gobi in Mongolia, others of the Kara Koum. Like the latter, it is dotted over with numerous tamarisk-trees, which have helped to consolidate the sand-hills. The wind and the shrub are at war with each other, the latter seeking to retain by means of its roots the moving surface of the desert, clutching, as it were with tentacles, little heaps of sand

and solidifying them, while the dust whirls round and the wind
converts it into a diminutive piece of artillery for besieging the
fortress. The pools are very numerous, lending to the plants
the sustenance of their moisture, and making the struggle less
unequal.

Coming to our first halt, we are advised to make to our
right, in a westerly direction, and we thread our way between
pools and pieces of water which remind one of fragments of
river which have suddenly come to a stop, for, when the
wind ruffles the water, one would imagine that it was flowing,
while when the wind drops it is still. But our horizon, up
to the present rather narrow, opens out; and the plain upon
which we enter is, as we are told, that of Koul toukmit Koul.
We see green *djiddas* of a very respectable size, while the
prickly broom waves its white tufts in the depression of the
soil, and between the low sand-hills runs a fine stream of clear
water glistening in the sunlight. This is the Tarim, which flows
along, as if fatigued by its long journey, towards the Lob Nor.
One can guess without much difficulty that a large lake, or a
number of pools, will be formed, for this river has no outlet into
the ocean.

Marching away from the Tarim, in the afternoon we arrive
at Aktarma, indicated in the desert by groups of poplars. A
herd of cattle announce our approach in a very disagreeable
manner, for they make a stampede in front of us, raising a column
of dust. They are animals of very small stature, and exceed-
ingly agile. We see men cultivating small patches of ground
impregnated with salt, not far from the score or so of huts which
constitute what is one of the most important towns of the Tarim.
These huts, made of reeds twisted into hurdles and mud, are for
the present deserted.

The chief of Aktarma, surrounded by his council, offers us
some very insipid melons, and inquires after our health. These

people are very frightened and suspicious, like the true savages they are; they have round heads and eyes, appearing to be the produce of unions between the most divergent tribes, all that they have in common being their savage and poverty-stricken mien.

CROSSING AN ARM OF THE TARIM AT ÁRKAN ON AN IMPROVISED RAFT (*p.* 69).

One would imagine them to be outlaws who had come from all parts, and who had settled here from weariness of wandering. They assert that they are Kalmucks by descent, but they speak Turkish. Abdullah, who wants to ingratiate himself with them, says that he is himself a Kalmuck, and that the Emir Timour was also a Kalmuck, whence it is to be concluded, judging by the tone of our interpreter, that this nation has possessed at least two great men—the Emir Timour, long since defunct, and Abdullah, our interpreter, the greediest of created beings, who ask them to give him some melons for his own consumption, and who will fall ill from eating too many.

October 16.—We halt all to-day. As the village remains deserted, the news of our arrival has, perhaps, frightened away the people of Aktarma. But it would appear that at this season the population migrates with its flocks and herds to the banks of the Tarim and its pools, men, women, and children fishing, shooting, and drying fish for the winter, while the cattle and sheep are feeding.

Beyond the wood men are at work digging the ground with the same simple implement which one meets with among all primitive peoples, consisting of two pieces of wood. The savages invented it first of all for delving into the earth and robbing it of its treasures. Here the people grow wheat, but not enough for their food ; they have therefore, to go and buy more at Kourla, where they sell sheepskins, dried fish, and a coarse sort of cloth. They grow a little barley for their horses, which, though not numerous, are sturdy and good for their size.

October 17.—The plain across which we are travelling, with its grey October sky, forms a typical Pomeranian landscape, and one might fancy oneself on the shores of the Baltic or of the North Sea. The horizon is flat, water extends everywhere, and the lowlands seem to be floating on the surface, while the banks of the river are too low to regulate its course. It seems as though a mere scratch would suffice to open a way for the Tarim. The stream is constantly overflowing, or rather it spreads out and forms pools or lakes in a hundred different spots, as is evidenced by the name of the village of Yangi Koul (the "new lake"). We approach this place along a dusty road, shaded by reed-beds and thorns, and running through ground with a good deal of salt on the surface ; and we have to wind in and out so as to avoid the water. The village is perched upon the slope of a sandhill on the opposite bank, and the walls of the houses, very irregularly built, look as if they were slipping down towards the river. Our arrival brings out the whole population, which comes to take a good look

9

at us while we are having our tea. The women alone do not cross the stream, which is nearly 500 feet wide, but men and boys jump into the water and tuck up their clothes so as to reach the mole of sand which lines the course of the Tarim. The well-to-do, who have boots or shoes on their feet, get themselves carried across, or come over in canoes. They bring presents with them, including fish, both fresh and preserved. One lad has brought a wild goose alive, and when, while refusing it, we make him a present, he shows our gift to the others, and the ice is broken.

The natives come so close that I have time to examine them, and can see that they are a mixture of all races, with noses and eyes of all shapes and colours, as in any large town in the West. I detect some typical Kirghis, thick-set, with scarcely perceptible eyes, salient cheek-bones, and scanty beards; Sarthians with finer figures, and black, bushy beards, while grey eyes are not rare. A fair man with a very fresh complexion and light eyes wears a turned-up cap on his head, and the Siberians themselves are struck by his resemblance to a Russian. Moreover, we are told that the Russians have been here.

Our presence excites the greatest curiosity, and the canoes are kept busy, bringing the whole of the male population; while the women, clustering on the opposite bank, watch the spectacle, and doubtless wish that the etiquette of their sex did not prevent them from coming across. These people bring us some excellent melons and boiled fish, the meal being hurriedly prepared for us. When we eat, the crowd kneel down and watch us with almost reverent interest. They exchange remarks in a low tone, and appear very pleased to see us, but one of them observes: " Had you been Chinese, we should have made off." After making a few presents, we encamped some distance farther on, on high ground, which is rather drier.

October 18.—We traverse Ouloug Koul, where the chief, a Kirghis by descent, accords us a hearty reception in his house, made of withes plastered with mud. He has some furniture in his house, including a wooden X on which the Koran is placed, a mat which he unrolls, and which serves both as cloth and table, cushions made out of real silk taken from the stem of the *tchiga* (*asclepias*), and bags made of a sort of wild hemp which is very abundant in this region. He drinks his tea out of Kashgar cups, and has several wives, being altogether an important personage. Although we decline his proffered sheep, we offer him in return a present; it is always well to encourage generous intentions when one is travelling.

We were able to observe here the action of the wind upon the sands of the Tarim: they are being slowly driven towards the north-west, for the prevailing wind is the south-east, though one from the south-west is said to blow occasionally. The aged chief who gives us this information tells us that the people pay a tax every year to the Chinese, he acting as intermediary between the former and the chief at Kourla. The impost is levied upon the crops and the stock, a tenth of the former and a fortieth part of the latter.

October 19.—The route does not vary. Whenever we quit the banks of the river we return to the desert, through plantations where the *tougrak* trees, exuding their sap, which the natives employ as soap, lift their contorted heads, and past undulating sandhills driven along by the wind, but at so slow a pace that the natives do not notice their advance until after many years. The incidents of the route are the occasional securing of a bird or a mammal, which goes to enrich our collection. Game is fairly abundant. First it is an antelope which springs up within shot, and is bagged, or our menu is varied by a hare or by Mongolian pheasants. Then we see a wolf, at first mistaken for a dog, stealing through the rushes, or the fresh trace of a tiger, which makes us take extra precautions at night. We come across European birds, too, such as fieldfares and larks,

while there is no lack of waterfowl. We have excellent camping-
ground, though the water is often bad, and not a day passes that
it does not make some of our men ill. They are forbidden to
drink water on the road, unless it is running, and even in that
case it is necessary to be very careful, for there are rapid
rivers which are more or less poisoned by the vegetable matter
in their beds, and by other plants which, growing on the banks,
die and fall in, undergoing decomposition and sowing the germs
of disease.

October 20.—A strong wind from the south-west brings a
little snow by way of warning that winter is at hand, and as we
sit round the fires at night the conversation turns upon the lofty
plateaus. Our interpreter in his vanity exaggerates the difficulties
of the route, for, as he is the only person who has gone through
a winter in these regions, he regards himself as a being of some
special essence. In the village of Tchigali we halt in the hut of
the chief. This village received its name from the abundance
of *tchigas* which the natives found when they settled here.
Wherever we go we encounter this plant, as well as the poplar,
the tamarisk, and the jujube-tree, and it gives a special character
to the valley of the Tarim.

October 21.—Before entering the desert, which has to be
crossed to get to Aïriligane, we go through regular fields of
tchiga. Of this the natives weave garments, the work being
always executed by women. The grains of the "silk plant," as
the *asclepias* of Europe is called, are surmounted by a silky
substance as soft to the touch as the finest velvet. Cushions are
manufactured from it, and it also makes a very soft bed for
children ; and when the dark and hard pod which contains the
grains is pressed, these emerge all at once in the shape of a bouquet
of great delicacy, as under the influence of a magician's wand.

October 22.—The event of to-day is the visit of a chief who
offers us presents consisting of melons, fish, onions, and carrots.

The carrots excite general enthusiasm, it being a long time since we had seen any of these excellent vegetables.

October 23.—We are still in the desert, and can see the Tarim flowing lazily along between its banks, all white with salt. We kill an enormous wild boar and some gazelles. The day is a magnificent one, after a minimum of 16° of frost at night, whereas during the day the temperature rises to 79° in the shade. The sky is overcast, and with the aspect of autumn we have the warmth of spring.

October 24.—Once more we are on the banks of one of the branches of the Tarim, and have no difficulty in constructing two rafts, one with a treble row of trunks of trees, the other with canoes brought to us by the natives, who are more wretched-looking than those who live higher up the river, more suspicious, and more savage. They are amused and alarmed at a mere nothing, and even our camels inspire them with such terror that they will not go near them.

The men of Arkan (this being the name of the place) are poor wretches all in rags, dressed in pieces of coarse cloth and fragments of a wadded coat, having on their feet *abarcas*, boots without any heels, or strips of stuff wound round their legs. They are of a very marked type, being small, dark, and very agile, showing little muscle, with skinny legs, and the calf high up towards the knee. They have broad faces, salient cheek-bones, and small round eyes of a dark colour, while one is struck by the long nose, coming down to a chin ending in a very scanty beard. Their cheeks are hollowed as if by hunger, their mouths very large, with the corners puckered down, and with thick over-lapping lips. Their necks are long and thin like those of the cormorants, which they resemble in the sense that they are in search of food from the hour of their birth. Their teeth, as a rule, are yellow, decayed, short, and worn sideways from gnawing at dried meat and munching grain. They are much amused at seeing us sneeze when we take some of the yellow snuff which they are constantly thrusting up their nostrils.

Savage and devoid of intelligence as they look, they have their code of honour. The Dungan camel-driver abuses them because they have pushed one of the camels into the water by their awkward movements, so they steer clear of him, heap curses on his head, and intimate their intention of going away. They will not do anything for him, and we are compelled to intervene and explain that he is only hired by us, and that in reality it is for us they are working. So they set to work again, but only on the condition that the Dungan keeps away from them.

It so happens that this morning, by way of punishing them for some careless act, Parpa took a stick and beat some of them, whereupon, instead of being angry, they offered excuses and promised to behave better. I asked one of their greybeards the meaning of this.

" Why do you say nothing to Parpa and get angry with the Dungan ? "

" Parpa is a Mussulman, a *sunni*, like ourselves."

" But the Dungan is a *sunni* too."

" We do not believe it, for he wears a pigtail like a Chinese; he speaks their language, and knows nothing of ours, except insults. Whereas Parpa is one of our acquaintances, he speaks our language and does not insult our mothers or the tombs of our fathers. He beat the men who made such a stupid blunder, and he was quite right. He is not a Chinese with hair falling down his back, and, besides, blows are not like the words which proceed from an evil heart."

As a matter of fact, the stick is commonly used for chastisement in these Eastern countries, and there is nothing ignominious in the injuries which it inflicts. Insults, on the other hand—and I mean thereby the curses upon relatives, ancestors, and tombs, uttered with the object of dishonouring the person at whom they are levelled—are rarely forgiven.

October 26.—Having got the whole of the caravan across, we encamped to-day in a wood at Talkitchin, a name which signifies "the small poplar" in the dialect of the country. The scenery is much the same, and directly one leaves the banks of the river one is in the desert with the tamarisk-tree, the *tchiga*, and tufts of reeds growing in its salt soil.

As I walk through the wood I observe that if it has been able to resist the desert it has not escaped the effects of time, for the leaves have been stripped from the trees earlier than they would have been if there had been much vigour in them, and the branches of the poplars are much twisted and bent. The trunks are either split or are devoid of bark, the ground is strewed with dead branches, and the roots, laid bare to the air, seem to have no hold on the ground. Seen from a distant elevation, these trees present the forlorn aspect of an abandoned vineyard, and the meagre trunks, devoid of a single branch, rear their heads like the poles in a hop field which has been allowed to go out of cultivation. The effect of all I see around me is to depress the imagination: the sand is so shifting that the footprints made in it are effaced in a moment; there is no sign of life; the pale sun goes down in a grey sky which it scarcely tinges with gold, while the silence is so complete that one can almost hear one's arteries beating.

The old Kirghis, Imatch, indulges in some very comical reflections about the camels, of which he is very fond, as, indeed, he is of all animals, taking care that the horses and dogs are not left without food. His only failing is that he has a very coarse tongue, and a boundless store of rich invective. He points out to me that the *kouirouk* (tail) of the sheep is not so thick as in the Ili, this being a proof that the pasturage is poor. There is nothing better than the fat of the sheep's tail.

October 27.—After a march through the sand, we encamped a little way beyond the ruined fortress constructed by Yakoob Beg, and of which the four crenellated walls still standing serve as a refuge in bad weather. The spot where we encamped is called Bougou Bashi, Bougou being the name given by the natives to the stags, which are pretty numerous in this country, while Bashi means head, the Tarim making a sharp bend, which is very like the head of a stag surmounted by his two horns.

October 28.—We direct our steps southward, delighted at the thought of entering the region of Lob. As we advance the aspect of the country changes, vegetation becoming rarer, while the trees have disappeared; the shrubs and plants are scantier, and the hillocks further apart, and frequently separated by the smooth surface of the *takirs*. There are traces of evaporation everywhere.

We take a south-south-westerly direction, with the wind at our backs. Quitting the banks of the Tarim for good, the desert becomes more and more in keeping with its name. All of a sudden we can see the glistening of water, a large sheet of which extends to our left, forming numerous creeks. Overhead thousands of birds are flying in clouds, while others allow themselves to be carried along the surface of the water by the wind, but at a considerable distance from the low banks, which are bare, coated with salt, and devoid of the thick belt of reeds which is to be found on most lakes. Further on is another sheet of water, and when we ascend a hillock we can distinguish an endless chain of them, with their sandhills, salt-coated shores, and water-fowl.

One of the guides says this region is the Lob, another that it is Kara Bourane; but it is really called the "Black Tempest," being the extreme west of the Lob.

The stream which runs in a current through this stagnant water is the Tchershène Darya, which comes down from the high table-lands to the north. It is not so broad as the Tarim, and a bridge of very modest size enables us to cross it, and to encamp in the island formed by it, the grass being good for the horses and camels.

The village of Lob is not far off, and the inhabitants come to

A NATIVE OF LOB.

pay us a visit. These starved and feeble-looking people offer to sell us smoked fish, and duck which they have snared, and a few presents soon make them friendly. They tell us that Petzoff, the Russian traveller, is expected shortly, and that the Chinese have

10

spread the report that smallpox is raging in the region of the Tchershène, so that the inhabitants of Tcharkalik have made up their minds to take flight before the Russians arrive. In this country smallpox terrifies the population, causing them to disperse in all directions, and even to abandon the sick.

October 29.—After having slowly steered our way through the marshes, we again see the bare plain in the desert. To the south we can distinguish a tall peak rising out of the mist, like an island in the sky, and the guide, pointing to it with his whip, says, "Altyn Tagh, the mountain of gold!" It is the first of the mountain walls which bar access to the high table-lands; as we look at it it vanishes like a dream.

We trot along a narrow, rough path, hewn, so to speak, out of the soil wherein the feet of men and beasts have worked a series of holes some distance apart. The path gets smoother, and at last we enter a tamarisk wood, while the poplars are still green and the air warm as in spring; thus we enter the oasis of Tcharkalik. Here there is abundance of irrigation, and the fields are well cultivated. There are peach and apricot trees, and even vines, with hedgerows enclosing the fields, and the presence of huts and cottages reminds one a little of the gardens outside large cities, like Marseilles.

We are very well received by the elders of the village of Tcharkalik, who bring us a profusion of melons, peaches, and grapes, and have some cakes of new bread baked for us; and in our delight at having reached the end of our second main stage, we sacrifice a whole hecatomb of these good things.

CHAPTER IV.

EXPLORATION OF THE LOB NOR.

(BY PRINCE HENRY OF ORLEANS.)

A Region of Salt—On the Tarim again—Abdallah—Residence of the Chief—His Family—
Wild Camels—Another Abdallah—Lost in the Darkness—More about Wild Camels—
Waterfowl—An Exchange—Disappearance of a Lake—Down the Tarim in Canoes—
Youtchap Khan—Another Native Type—Kumshap Khan—Straddling a River at Its
Mouth—At Eutin—Ichthyophagists—A Native Legend—Probable Causes of the Drying
up of the Lake—Native Customs—Festivities—Back to the First Abdallah—Tchaï—A
Couple of Good Shots—A Moonlight March—At Tcharkalik Once More.

WE had already been four days at Tcharkalik, and were not nearly
ready to start, having to engage men of the district in place of
our Russians who were returning home, to get in provisions
for the winter, to mend clothes, and to make coverings for pro-
tecting the feet from the cold. All this takes time, and as
Bonvalot had promised to see after this, Father Dedeken and
myself, who could be of no service at Tcharkalik, availed
ourselves of the compulsory halt of the caravan to explore the
Lob Nor, starting on the 3rd of November.

Our horses had already travelled more than 600 miles since
we left Djarkent, and as we had still to tax their powers a great
deal, we left them to rest at Tcharkalik. Riding some animals
which we hired there, thick-set ponies, with deep chests, short
and heavy necks, and small heads, and that seemed able to stand
plenty of work, we found it as much as we could do to hold them
at the start. Abdullah, who takes, as meant for himself, the
attention which these stallion ponies bestow on the mare he is
riding, casts a patronising look at the natives who have come
to see us off. He is in his element going to the Lob Nor, for he
thinks he will be able to do as he likes with us, and keep us well
away from the villages, while he remains there eating, smoking,
and flirting with the young ladies of the place. A smile of

self-satisfaction plays over his face as he abandons himself to his reveries. In front of him Father Dedeken and Barachdin, both keen for the chase, are discounting their coming triumphs, while behind them Couznetzoff, bent double, has as much as he can do to keep his pony in order, and, when he can find a quiet moment, wipes his spectacles, and hopes we shall not kill too many birds for him to stuff.

A little way behind us come half a dozen small donkeys, accompanied by two Mussulmans from Tcharkalik, and carrying some provisions and our beds, which consist of a piece of felt and a coverlet. Abdullah declares that we shall find very good houses, and that it is useless to encumber ourselves with a tent. We have also two small barrels of water and a little dry wood.

When we left the encampment at 9 a.m. the weather was cold, but there was no wind or cloud. Still the sky was overcast, having that iron-grey tint which I have often noticed on the Teraï in Nepaul, and which is caused by a mist intercepting a portion of the light.

M. Bonvalot came a little way with us through the oasis of Tcharkalik, as far as the limit of the desert. The arrangement was that if we found the shooting in the Lob Nor anything out of the common, we were to let him know and he would join us. If not, we were to rejoin him in about a week.

As far as a small hillock where we took tea when coming from Lob, the road is the one over which we have already travelled, but we then turn to the right—that is, to the north-east. All day we go through the desert, with nothing but sand in view, in some places level and smooth as a carpet, in others wrinkled and raised into ridges which are close together, like so many petrified waves. Sometimes, too, we notice small cavities in the soil, which are half full of saline crystallisations. These are *géodes* forming under our very eyes, and it is probably to all this salt that are due the mirages which are constantly tantalizing us in this arid region, where the passage of the caravans has traced a rough sort of road which has been hardened by the drought, and which winds along in the distance like a furrow traced by the hand of man. One might imagine oneself to be transported into the scenery of the moon, and we really begin to forget where we are. Our march soon becomes horribly monotonous, and we cease singing and even talking, the solitude being quite contagious, and the general silence only broken by the footfall of the horses when they are crossing dried-up ponds and their hoofs break through the crust. We are only aroused from our reveries by meeting with a caravan, and when we shake off our torpor we have the feeling of returning to the domain of the real which is experienced by the sleeper who wakes up with a start.

From time to time we pass migrants from the Lob Nor who are going to spend the winter at Tcharkalik, with their luggage, their dwellings, and their furniture loaded on the backs of a few donkeys, and of their wives. In the midst of one of these convoys I am particularly struck by one family. The woman has a piece of felt on her back, with a gun slung across her shoulders, and she is driving the donkey along with a stick, while the husband follows quietly nursing a child in his arms. He does not seem to be the least astonished at meeting us, and continues his journey without even looking round; he would not be a whit more surprised if death were to overtake him, for he is a Mussulman, and knows that "it is written."

Despite the sameness of the route, time passes quickly, and we have to think about encamping. We calculate that we have come about twenty-five miles, and though we are still in the midst of the desert, our guides are not in the least at a loss to fasten up our horses, after having unloaded them. They make small holes in the ground and put the halters into them, then filling these holes up with sand and treading them down. This mode of fastening horses offers much more resistance than one

might be inclined to think.   Having spread out our pieces of felt,
we light the dry wood we have brought with us, and our frugal
meal of *caverdak*,* washed down with tea, is soon over.   It is
not long before we roll ourselves up in our rugs, and, with the
desert for a mattress, the sky for a ceiling, and the moon for a
night-light, we desire nothing better, especially as we are very
sleepy.

November 4.—We are awoke at break of day by a deep
murmur over our heads.   It is a rhythmical sound, similar to
that of the paddles of a steamer as they strike the water,
and it is produced by flocks of birds which are flying southward.
The season is advancing, and it is time for them to get away from
the cold.

And very cold it is, the thermometer marking only five degrees
above zero.   Being anxious to start so as to re-establish our
circulation, we do not lose much time in folding up our beds,
preparing our tea, and loading our donkeys.   Some wild geese
that had got left behind are standing in long rows upon the sand,
and seen from the distance they look gigantic, and give the idea
of troops drawn up in battle array.   We, no doubt, present a still
more formidable appearance to them, for as soon as they catch
sight of us, they utter the most discordant cries and fly away,
forming immense triangles in the air with the apex in front.

The sun bursts out at last, and, though rather behind time, he
makes up for this by revealing a quite unlooked-for spectacle.
The ground is covered with the seeds of reed grass brought hither
by the wind, and these seeds, white and silky, sparkle like an
infinity of small stars in the horizontal rays.   It seems as if the
desert was ashamed of its horrible nudity, and that, in order to
conceal it from our sight, it had borrowed from the star of day its
rarest jewels and its most dazzling stones.   Beside the brilliant
diamonds, large round sapphires of a deep and splendid blue are

---

* *Carerdak* is meat cut up into very small pieces and fried in the pan.

represented by small circular pools, which owe their sombre tints to the saltness of the water. These pools of water indicate the vicinity of a river, and it is not long before we regain the course of the Tarim, which is fifty feet broad, with a limpid but shallow current, flowing slowly between two sandy banks, which are covered in places with reeds.

Its course will guide us in future along our route, for we have to follow it pretty closely, putting to flight now and again herds of gazelles which have come to drink of its waters. But they are very wild, and we do not succeed in bringing any down.

The sun is rapidly sinking beneath the horizon, yet we see no trace of dwellings. The thirty versts which, as the guide told us this morning, separated us from the village of Abdallah, seem to us very long ones; we have covered, indeed, quite double the distance, and it is night when we reach four or five wretched reed hovels. Can this be the village of Abdallah? Where are the houses built of stone, or, at all events, of earth, which he told us about. Where, too, are the trees, the wood of which was to give us warmth? and why should he have dissuaded us from bringing our tents?

These are questions which we should have liked to put to Abdullah, but it is cold and late, and all that we can do is to content ourselves with what we have got, and settle ourselves in as comfortably as possible, taking care to be on our guard in future against the information supplied by our interpreter. While our people are unloading the horses and donkeys, the natives emerge from their miserable hovels, and with many salaams beg us to accept their hospitality.

We enter one of these huts, the earthen floor of which is covered in places with old bits of felt, while in the centre a cavity surrounded by flat stones serves as a fireplace. In the corner are sacks of corn and an old cartridge box, the latter being a *souvenir* of Prjevalsky's visit. This is all the furniture, and on the walls, constructed of reeds, are hung long guns with powder flasks, so that the inmates are given to shooting. The ceiling is made out of the branches of trees brought from Tcharkalik, the interstices being filled up with osiers, and a space is left over the hearth to let the smoke escape. Bits of cloth are stretched from one beam to another to prevent the droppings from the swallows' nests from falling on to the ground. These birds are held in great respect.

This is the residence of a chief, and having inspected the house, I proceed to examine the figures of our hosts, lighted up by the fire made of the reeds and dry bushwood. In the foreground, close to the hearth, crouches a little old man, very bent and wrinkled. He resembles some of the Tarantshis whom we saw at Kourla. With a more or less automatic motion of his lower jaw, he raises his white beard to the level of his hooked nose, this movement being all the easier because he has no teeth. This is Abdou Kérémata, who might be any age between 95 and 105, and as he is the chief of the family, the *baba*,* he is, as such, held in great respect.

Around him are his sons, the youngest of whom is at least forty. They are all devoted to the chase—tall men, clad in sheepskins tied round the waist with a belt, with fur caps on their heads, and wearing sandals made of the skins of donkeys or wild camels. Their features show that they are not of pure blood, the forehead being narrow and the eyes more or less elongated, but not raised at the corners, as is the case with the yellow race. As a rule, they scarcely open their eyelids; the nose is large, and, usually, rather hooked, the lips thick and inclined to turn up, and the hair coarse and scanty. Such are their general characteristics, to which I may add one peculiarity which I noticed everywhere in the Lob Nor. The people get wrinkled from their early youth, and their faces show signs of this all over —on the forehead, round the eyes, under the cheeks, and at the

* Grandfather.

corners of the mouth, producing an air of premature age and of grimacing which makes men who are, taking them altogether, rather handsome, appear very ugly. The family of Abdou Kérémata invite us to come round the fire ; they pour out tea for us, and bring us the best bits of mutton—that is, the breast and

THE VILLAGE OF ABDALLAH.

the loin. Our hosts keep complete silence, only a word here and there being exchanged in an undertone while we are eating. In the next room women are rocking cradles to a tune which suggests the dull sound of a pestle being worked in a mortar, while at a respectful distance from the hearth children nearly naked look from us to their fathers, and keep quite silent out of timidity.

"Allah Akbar!" exclaims Abdullah, passing his hands through his beard, while the guests express their satisfaction by some incongruous sounds. The meal being finished, it is time to

11

talk, and there is a piece of good news for us, for some animals have just been eaten by a tiger, so perhaps we may have a chance of tracking him.

With regard to the wild camels, our hosts have killed four in the last two years, but they have cut up their skins. In telling us this, they guess that we should want them whole, with the head and the feet. The only Europeans who have come here before wanted them like this, so they suppose that "the people of the West attach great importance to these skins; perhaps they extract valuable remedies from them."

Whatever may be their object, travellers never come to the Lob Nor without inquiring about the wild camels. One of the men present provided Prjevalsky with some. The tariff has always been sixty roubles and an article of European manufacture for a complete skin. But we spoil the market, at the risk of incurring the displeasure of those who come after us. We are pressed for time, the wild camels are only to be found some way to the east, and a fortnight is soon gone; so we promise seventy roubles for each skin, and promise the men a gratuity even if they do not kill any. Abdullah goes bail for us, and in doing so incurs little risk, as he does not intend to return to the Lob Nor sooner than he can help.

November 5.—We are in the saddle before sunrise, following for another four miles the Tarim, which runs between high banks, and halting again at a fresh village with five or six reed huts similar to the one we have just left. This also is called Abdallah, and all that it has more than the first is a pole, to which we fasten our horses, on the "public square." Hospitality is offered us by a native about forty years old, with a straight, big nose, thick but not protruding lips, and a very wrinkled skin. He has a very genial face, and breathes an air of jollity which is quite communicative. This is Kunshi Khan Beg, whose portrait has already been drawn by Prjevalsky, who was his guest for more than a month. Like Abdou Kérémata, he is the head of a family of hunters, and he promises to do what he can to procure us the skin of a wild camel; and when he hears our proposals, he induces five of his men to get ready for a start into the desert. Other natives are longing to get on to the track of the tiger referred to above.

While Abdullah was interpreting our promises, garnished with some of his own inventions, Father Dedeken went up to two Mongolian *yourtes* (tents), close to which five camels were picketed. These tents were inhabited by five very dirty lamas, who were preceding the Khan of the Kalmucks on his return from Lhassa. As we know that they have just traversed the highlands of Thibet, upon which we are about to enter, they may perhaps be able to give us some useful information. Father Dedeken accordingly calls out to them in Chinese, "Amour sen! Amour sen béné!* Come and take tea with us." They understand perfectly what is said to them, and accept the invitation with pleasure. The pleasure, however, is scarcely reciprocal, for they smell atrociously. Nor do they seem to understand this, as, the more I sheer off from them, the closer they come up to me. We feel that it will not do to be too particular, but we are poorly rewarded for our hardihood, for, while they drink our tea very readily, they will not tell us anything worth knowing, saying all they can to deter us from going on.

The rest of the day is employed in shooting in the vicinity. The water-fowl are pretty numerous, and they keep to small pools, which, as a rule, are circular, and are surrounded by a belt of reeds fifteen or twenty feet high, forming a regular forest; the ground is marshy, and covered in some places with rushes, which make the walking very bad. When one has got through these on to the bank, it is easy to have a double shot, but the birds all get up, and it is necessary to walk round the pond and go to the other

* Mongolian for "Good health."

side, or else pass on to the next. This is very fatiguing work, and so we soon return, after having seen a great deal of game, but no great variety of species. This is not the time of year when there is a great passage of birds, and, as we have not enough cartridges to amuse ourselves by making a big bag, we must only kill what we require for our collections and for food.

On returning to Abdallah, I utilised the few remaining hours of daylight to get on my pony and ride back over yesterday's route, in the hope of seeing some more gazelles. I did not see a single one, but I was so absorbed in looking about for them that I let night overtake me. In these regions it comes all of a sudden, without any twilight. With a carelessness without excuse in such a case, I had forgotten my compass. Only one resource was left to me, and that answered. I let the reins drop on my horse's neck, and he, after sniffing for a moment, set off without hesitation at a slow trot, and took me straight to the village, which I could not distinguish until I was within a hundred yards of it.

This nocturnal ride gave me an appetite, and I did justice to the meal which Kunshi Khan and his sons shared with us, for our host had offered us a sheep, a Tcharkalik melon, and ten small sandwiches similar to those made in Russia, and called *pirojki*. The secret of making them was taught his wife by a Russian Cossack, and, whatever may have been the motive which actuated him, we bless this unknown philanthropist and quaff a cup of tea to his health. During our dinner, a woman prepares in the same room a dish of Chinese macaroni. She is not good-looking, being of the same type as the men, but her head-dress gives her a more civilised air, while after the fashion of the Russian peasants, she covers her coarse black hair with a *fichu*, tied under the chin. One might imagine she was conscious of her ugliness, for she talked very little, and did not take her food at the same time as the men, who have not the slightest notion of gallantry. The children are prettier than their mother, not being

WOMEN OF ABDALLAH AND NATIVES OF THE LOB NOR, WITH IMPLEMENTS.

yet wrinkled, and there are some fine types among them; they are all nearly naked, and seem to be in excellent health. After they have had a good look at us, they withdraw into an adjoining room, followed by the women, who leave us alone with their husbands. The latter, having made a hearty meal, are in a good humour and ready to reply to the questions we put to them concerning their mode of life, their habits, and their pursuit of game. Wild camel, we are told, begin to be found six days to the north of Abdallah. In the summer they go up into the mountains, but they always return to the same spots, there being certain cantonments to which they are accustomed. They go about in troops, one male to fifteen or sixteen females, but it is only after terrific combats that the former becomes the undisputed lord of his harem. The females have two young in three years, and the male protects them until they are old enough to do without their mother's milk. It is very fatiguing and difficult to get near them, the only way being for the hunter to hide near the pond on the brink of which he has found their traces. He must be a very good shot, for having only a single-barrelled gun, he cannot get a second shot, and if the camel is only wounded, it will make off with its companions and he will never get near it again. The best season for this sport is the winter, for the water is nearly everywhere frozen over, so that the places where the camels come to drink are very few, and you are pretty sure of finding them.

As to whether these camels have always been wild or are descended from domesticated ones, our hosts assured us that they had always been wild. "Our forefathers and tradition," they said, "represent them as being so. Moreover, a domesticated camel cannot do without man, but comes after him. Every domestic animal has a wild antecedent, belonging to some secluded spot. The camel must have one like other animals.*

* The reader is probably aware that the wild camel is spoken of as far back as the fifteenth century in the deserts of Central Asia, and that the fact of its existence has

"When the chase has been successful it is very profitable, as the camel's skin is in great demand for boots, while the hair of the younger animals is fine and silky, and that of the older camels is close, and makes very good cloth. But only rich people like Kunshi Khan can organise these expeditions, as it is necessary to send several men on in advance, forward provisions, furnish animals for transporting them, which sometimes die; and altogether considerable risk has to be incurred."

It is much easier and less dangerous to capture water-fowl. Snares are set among the reeds, and during the season a single native, in the course of a single night, will take as many as fifteen ducks.* Swans are more profitable than ducks, coverlets and even clothing being made with their down. They are taken with snares, while in the winter they are decoyed by means of fish.

The chase and fishing form the staple industry of the inhabitants of Abdallah. They use nets similar to seines, and when the fish have been caught they are split in two, cleaned out, and then dried for use in winter. There are three varieties of fish, the most abundant of which has a thin and yellow skin like that of the tench, with a round mouth set off by appendages

---

been confirmed in the last fifty years, but has only been definitely proved since Prjevalsky brought back some skins of the animal, which is rather smaller than the domesticated kind, with thinner limbs and no callosities at the knees. These characteristics are not distinctive. The question as to whether the wild camel is the parent stock of the domesticated one, or whether, on the contrary, he descends from some tame camel, as has happened in Spain and more recently in Guiana, is not yet settled, nor is it likely to be yet a while.

* The swallows arrive at Abdallah in April, and leave again in September. A species of red duck, called here Turfan (in Chinese, *Choumi chizeu*, red beak), arrives in large numbers in February, and leaves in July. The geese arrive from the 20th to 28th February, remaining till the middle of March, and then going to Siberia. They return from September to October, remaining a month and then going southward. The swans arrive from the south at the end of July, remain throughout September, and then return south. They do not nest at the Lob Nor, because of the mosquitoes, according to the natives. The other ducks arrive towards the end of January, some remaining only ten days, but those which stay longer build their nests, like the puffins, the gulls, the herons, and other sedentary birds in the Lob Nor.

on each side; they are rarely more than twenty-two inches long.

The natives of Abdallah also eke out their livelihood by the rearing of stock, which they possess in large numbers. They do not till the ground, but they own some fields at Tcharkalik, which workmen cultivate for them, and they pay them in kind with a part of the crop and a few sheep. Altogether, the people of Abdallah are regarded as rich, and they are under the immediate protection of the Chinese—that is to say, the authorities of Turfau, to which they are attached, levy on them a tax which is equivalent to one rouble per horse, forty copecks per cow or ox, two roubles per hundred sheep, and nine skins of seals for the head-dress of the mandarins. In return for this, the Celestial Empire declares them to be its well-beloved children. But although they are Chinese subjects, they have not the characteristics of their masters, being less proud and more simple than the sons of Heaven. Before quitting us for the night, they show us in a very amusing way how preferable common sense is to conceited knowledge. In this instance common sense is represented by Kunshi Khan, and instruction by Abdullah, who is a savant by comparison, as he can speak four languages, and has a great opinion of himself. The former shows a stereoscope and a musical-box which Prjevalsky gave him. Abdullah thinks that if he were to send these two articles back by the Russians to his family at Djarkent, he would dazzle his compatriots, and appear a great man in their eyes, while Kunshi Khan says to himself that if he had Abdullah's wadded coverlet he should be very warm in the winter. The exchange is accordingly made, each thinking that he has got the best of the bargain. I know which of the two really has, and I shall ask our "intelligent" interpreter, later on, if he thinks that Kunshi Khan is nice and warm.

November 6.—We are anxious to get away to the Lob Nor,

12

and see the immense lake, the beginning of which we noticed near the village of Lob, and the surface of which, according to Abdullah, is dark with myriads of water-fowl.

" But," say the natives, " you are at the Lob Nor."

" What do you mean ?   Where, then, is the great lake ? "

" There is no great lake."

" Then what becomes of the Tarim ? "

" It gradually dwindles away and finally disappears."

" But Prjevalsky saw a lake which he compared to a small sea."

" No doubt, but since the Russian general came here, thirteen years ago, the water has run off, and the largest liquid surface is that which you saw near Lob.   Besides, there are no longer anything but small pools."

" Thank you.   We are quite ready to believe you, but we should like to see for ourselves what the state of things is, and we propose to go down the Tarim a little way."

In order to carry out this project, all we have to do is to embark, with our beds and a few provisions, on two large canoes hewn out of the trunk of a tree.   These canoes are about twenty feet by three, and they hold four men, including two natives, one in the bow and the other in the stern, who use their paddles much after the fashion of the Venetian gondoliers.   These boats are light, and not very steady, so the wary Abdullah suggests that we should follow the example of Prjevalsky, and tie them together, but his advice is not followed, time being short.   The weather is fine, we have a light westerly breeze in the poop, and we make rapid headway down stream, upon both banks of which are low hillocks of sand, with a few stunted tamarisk trees growing on them.   The Tarim is from twenty-two to twenty-five feet broad, dividing at places into two branches, and forming an eyot.   At one of these eyots we halt for a little, and are overtaken by boats that have come from Lob loaded with provisions for the winter.

A few miles farther on we come to Youtchap Khan, as four or five reed huts erected under a sandy hillock are called, the village having a small canal which was cut about fifteen years ago to let off the overflow of water.

At Youtchap Khan we make a fresh halt, to oblige Abdullah, who is not very fond of this sort of navigation, and the whole population comes out to have a look at us. The men are like those at Abdallah, but the women are even uglier, having snub noses, prominent cheek-bones, eyes almost on a level with the face, and large mouths some distance from the extremity of the nose, being altogether very much of the Mongolian type. Men and women receive us in very friendly fashion, and allow us to inspect their dwellings, and to photograph their implements, which are simple and few in number. The guns are the same as those we have seen before, with a single barrel, which is long, and has an iron prong attached to it. Spending most of their time in the chase, they breed a few sheep, like the people at Abdallah, and make use of the wool, which they comb out by stretching it upon a rope fastened to a wooden handle, and making the rope vibrate by means of a sort of mallet. When they have got the wool to the required degree of fineness, they roll it on to a spinning-wheel, formed by two parallel indentated wheels, the points of which are fastened together with pieces of string. Besides wool, they use for their clothing the bark of a variety of wild hemp (*tchiga*), which they root up with a hoe made of a triangular piece of iron, with a cane as the stick. They cut their wood with a primitive sort of hatchet, which consists of a fragment of iron fixed on to the extremity of a piece of bent wood. The corn is ground between two flat stones, each fastened in the middle to a piece of wood. They use pumpkins instead of gourds, while the skins of antelopes, with the hair taken off, dried, and scraped, are cut into long strips for making fishing-nets. Adding to these few articles of prime necessity a horse's tail for driving away the flies, and a reed mat which answers the purpose of a napkin, an exact idea may be formed of what is to be found in their dwellings.

Returning to our boats, we continue the descent of the Tarim, the sand banks of which continue as far as Kumshap Khan ("Dug out from the Sand"), which is another collection of reed-hovels. The inhabitants seem even more woebegone than the people already described, with nothing but a few pieces of ragged felt to barely cover them, while their enormous sheep-skin caps, the wool of which is mixed up with their unkempt hair, make their physiognomy seem all the more savage. Yet, beneath this repulsive exterior, we find them very amiable and friendly. They are nine families in all, with about sixty members, and we cannot refuse their invitation to stay a few minutes and take a cup of tea. The sides of the house we enter are covered with white patches produced by the damp, and as the interior is dirty, we are not sorry to be off.

The Tarim divides into two arms beyond Kumshap Khan, the greater part of the waters flowing to the left and forming a large marsh, with islets of sand rising above the surface here and there. At the rear of the village is a lake about 330 feet long, but not more than a foot or two deep, while beyond that are peat-bogs, salt-ponds, and strips of ground covered by a few stunted gorse bushes and reed-beds. At Kumshap Khan the sand banks come to an end, and the right arm of the Tarim, which continues to flow eastward, is only from seven to sixteen feet broad, its banks being scarcely visible, while the immense reeds which grow along them have their roots in the water. The stream, already so much shrunken, is still further diminished by the number of small furrows cut on the right bank by the natives to guard against inundations. The river winds very much, and we have difficulty in getting round some of the bends, owing to the length of our canoes, but our boatmen have

ON THE TARIM.

made up their minds to the inevitable, and they accompany the motion of their oars with a rhythmical song, ending with a sort of sigh which we all repeat in chorus. Soon we are navigating a stream about five feet wide; and, at the risk of wetting my feet, I cannot resist the temptation of standing astride one of the largest rivers of Central Asia at its mouth, and seeing it flow between my legs. In front, behind, on each side and above us, are nothing but bulrushes, with patches of sky on which stars are beginning to appear, for night is drawing on, and our mén advance but slowly, while our stomachs remind us that it is high time to find a place of rest.

All of a sudden, as if by enchantment, at the bend of the stream we come upon a little creek to the left, a clear space amid the rushes, a mead coming down to the bank, and on the bank a man! I do not know whether he or our party are the more surprised.

On jumping ashore, my first impulse is to give him a cordial shake of the hand, for a man represents to my mind inhabitants, a village, fire, and dinner. But I cannot help being angry with our boatmen for having deceived us, by saying that there was no village beyond Kumshap Khan.

I tell Abdullah to ask where we are.

"At Eutin."

"Did the boatmen know of this village?"

"Yes, they belong to it."

"Why did they not tell us of it?"

"They were afraid that we should steal their wives."

"Reassure them, and say that we only ask them to give us shelter, and that we do not mean them any harm."

Our men do as they are bid, and take us to the hamlet, the name of which means "a place that has been burnt," for the houses are built upon a small clearing made by a fire in the midst of the reeds. There is a population of about fifty. Our

boatmen had been away for several days, so their aged fathers
greet them by kissing them on both cheeks; while they, in their
turn, embrace their sons. We ingratiate ourselves with all the
inhabitants by buying one of the two village sheep which had
been fattened for the marriage of the chief's son, and as soon as
the animal has been killed and cut up, it is cooked, we sharing
the meal with our hosts. This is a great treat for them, as they
rarely taste meat more than once a year; and, in addition to
being too poor to afford it, they say that it would be bad for
them to eat it frequently. Perhaps this is another case of
" grapes being sour," but, in any case, it is certain that, like
certain peoples of Arabia, they are ichthyophagists, though they
eat duck as well as fish. In their view, as in that of the mediæval
monks, the flesh of ducks is not meat; though the motive for
holding this view may not be the same in the two cases. They
also eat the young sprouts of the reeds, and the roots of the wild
hemp, which they fry. I am delighted at their friendly feeling,
and take advantage of their loquacity and of Abdullah's good
humour to pursue the investigation which I began at Abdallah.
We shall probably not go any farther on the Lob Nor, or ever
return there, so it would be a pity to lose the opportunity of getting information with regard to regions of which so little is known.

Here, as in the other villages, we are seated in a circle round
the hearth, the fire being made of bundles of dried reeds. The
ends are lighted first, and the flame gradually consumes the
stalks, a little girl pushing the bundle farther in as it burns.
The flame is very vivid, and as we get a better light than we
should from a lamp, and are well warmed into the bargain, we
have nothing to complain of.

The bulk of our conversation is with an old woman, whose
skin is so wrinkled that it is scarcely possible to distinguish her
toothless mouth between her nose and her chin. According to
the custom of the country, her head is covered with a fichu; her

hands are mere skin and bones, and on one of her fingers is a ring with a small blue stone—a coloured pebble, which has probably been palmed off upon her by a Chinaman. From the frontiers of Siberia to Tonquin, and even beyond, it is safe to say: "Wherever there is a robbery, a Chinaman is in it." The old lady appears to be held in high esteem in her village, this being due to her age and to her musical talents; for whenever the conversation flags she takes up a two-stringed guitar and sings long legends to a monotonous, but soft and harmonious tune, relating the history of her ancestors, their origin, their struggles, their flight, and their return. She sings in a nasal, slow tone, in a Turkish dialect which Abdullah has difficulty in following. But one of our boatmen, who knows the Tcharkalik language, assists him, and, with the help of Father Dedeken and his Chinese, I succeed in noting down a good part of the legend, as follows :—

"Once upon a time, four kings ruled the country, which was very prosperous with its Mussulman inhabitants. These kings were : Attagout Agha (Agha is a title), residing at Kargalik* ; Nouniaz Agha, Mardjan Agha, both of whom resided at Gashar†, and Shèr Agha, at Mienshari, near Abdallah‡. Then came the Mongols, who entered upon a struggle with them. They massacred a portion of the male inhabitants, and as the others did not choose to remain as slaves, they fled with some of the women, and succeeded in escaping eastward, three days' march from Eutin.§

"There was still water there then, though now there is only saltpetre, but as the fugitives had no house, they dug down into the ground to make fire, whence the name of the place, Karakoutchoun (black chimneys). There they began to feed only on fish and ducks.

* Now Tcharkalik.
† Three days' march from Tcharkalik, on the route to Khotan.
‡ These places were towns, the ruins of which are still visible in the desert.
§ Some went as far as the Tsaïdam, where Prjevalsky discovered their tombs.

" They remained more than a century, but in the meanwhile the Mongols had gone away, after having destroyed everything, and the exiles, driven from their new colony by the drought, gradually returned to the west.

" Some went along the banks of the Tarim, between Kourla and Lob. Others proceeded as far as the former site of Kargalik, the name of which they had forgotten. Seeing ruins, they re-excavated them in search of treasure, but the Mongols had carried off everything, and the exiles found nothing but a spinning-wheel. So they gave the name of Tcharkal, which means spinning-wheel, to the town which they built.

" The chase and the rearing of stock sufficed for their needs until the arrival of an aged chief from Khotan, Ismail Ata*, who offered to teach them tillage. His offer being accepted, he brought several companions with him. And now differences arose between the former owners of the soil and the Khotanese; and the latter have many sons, who take in marriage the daughters of the former. But our race has always remained intact, and has not been subjected to any mixture of blood."†

She then abandons the domain of history for that of romance, and her improvisations, which seem to captivate the attention of her hearers, have less interest for us. I prefer learning all I can about the Lob Nor, and question those next to me.

I am told that it was also by exiles on their return from Karakoutchoun that the little villages along the banks of the Tarim in the Lob Nor were founded. Ata (the aged father) was born at Karakoutchoun sixty-eight years ago, and thirty-five years ago founded the hamlet of Eutin. Beyond Eutin, going in the direction of Karakoutchoun, there are two villages : Karakoyuk and Deutchmé, the latter being already uninhabited, for the water

---

* We passed a night under his roof.

† She forgets that a good many of the people who came from Karakoutchoun took back their wives, although they had borne children or were heavy with child to the Mongols, their masters.

has run off, the reeds have disappeared, and their places are taken by sand and salt. Karakoyuk will soon be abandoned, as its two last inhabitants are collecting their wretched belongings before leaving, and the people of Eutin are on the point of migrating westward.

The fishermen are taking refuge in the oasis of Tcharkalik, and are becoming tillers of the soil. The inhabitants of the Lob Nor, like the waters of the Tarim, are gradually withdrawing; the hovels are falling in, the hamlets are disappearing, and their very sites are invaded by giant reeds, which, in turn, no longer having the water needed to nourish them, are drying up and withering away. Then will begin the slow but certain work of the sand, which will come and cover the ruins of ancient cities, the remnants of villages, the houses whether of mud or of wood, the withered rushes, and the dead reeds, spreading over all this district a vast pall which it will be impossible to raise, for the sand will have buried what is now the Lob Nor in everlasting oblivion.

Already it has partly done its work, for the Lob Nor as we see it is not as it was in Prjevalsky's time, and the Russian general himself could not find the lake* which is marked upon the old Chinese maps, and the existence of which is confirmed by the old woman we were talking with. According to the tradition handed down from generation to generation, there was at one time a vast inland sea here, without any sedges or reeds. The old men of the tribe have themselves seen large lakes, though nothing to compare with the sea which they have heard spoken of. One of them says that the water recedes every day, and that it must be absorbed by the saltpetre. To this reason, which may be to some extent valid, I will add another—for the last ten years

* It is this great lake which, according to the tradition, has given the Lob Nor its name—Lob being a local word signifying wild animals. It was already given to the district when the Kalmuck caravans traversed it, and they added the Mongolian word Nor (great lake).

Chinese Turkestan, which was formerly the theatre of constant
civil wars, seems to have been pacified, at all events for a time, and
the inhabitants are taking advantage of this truce to devote themselves to the cultivation of the fields, which they had been compelled for some time to abandon. In order to irrigate their fields
they have diverted part of the waters of the Tarim, which are thus
lost in irrigations or artificial inundations; while crops like cotton
or rice, which require a great deal of moisture, are becoming more
extensive each year, and consequently the body of water brought
into the Lob Nor district is very considerably less.

In reply to our questions as to whether they enjoy good
health, and to what complaints they are subject, they reply that
their mode of life is a healthy one, and that epidemics are rare.
They do not know what it is to have smallpox, and are never
subject to the ulcers which are so frequent in the East. When
they reach a certain age, they generally live to be old; but among
young children the mortality is at the rate of one in five. They
tell us that the children have no malady, but "they will not keep
alive," and this is the best explanation we can get. The complaints from which adults suffer come chiefly from the damp—
either a chill, or rheumatism in the legs, which sometimes partially
paralyses old people; or else a disease of the bones. This is often
the consequence of rheumatism, and the old dame tells us that
when this disease of the bones attacks a woman who is with child,
she is sure to die.

When a marriage takes place, the father of the bridegroom
gives the father of the bride ten bundles of wild hemp, ten packets
of dried fish, ten cups of fish-oil, a stew-pan, twenty or thirty
loaves of bread, from fifty to a hundred ducks, a flint and steel,
and a boat. This is the ordinary tariff, the rich giving a few
additional fish or ducks. The eatables are, moreover, consumed
at the wedding feast. The reader might gather from this list of
presents that the principal occupation is shooting and fishing.

They can neither read nor write, and the traditions of the country are handed down by word of mouth from one generation to another. Some of these traditions comprise lofty ideas; for these people, though very poverty-stricken, are not savages. They are religious, and declare themselves proud of being Mahometans —this constituting one of the reasons for their contempt of the

THE LATTER END OF THE TARIM.

Chinese and Mongols, whom they describe as people having "no book." Their religious practices consist in listening to a few verses of the Koran recited by one of the elders of the tribe; their ceremonies are simple, being limited to burials. When a man dies, his hands and feet are tied, and if his family has any cloth, a new garment is made for him; but if not, he is dressed in an old one. An elder recites a few Mussulman prayers, and the corpse is placed on a stretcher made of reeds and osiers; it is then covered with rushes, and placed in the midst of the reeds, and the relatives cut more reeds and heap them on the dead body; a pole bearing a bit of paper at the end is fixed in the ground, and so the ceremony ends.

All along the lower course of the Tarim the mode of pro-
cedure is the same, with this slight difference, that in certain
places a small hillock of sand for the pile of reeds is substituted.

We have been conversing for a couple of hours, and before
going to rest the aged Ata asks us in turn a question—he cannot believe that we are not Russians, and he wants to know why
we do not come to deliver them from the Chinese. We promise
him we will do what we can, and, in wishing each other good-
night we cordially agree in expressing our detestation of all the
Chinese. The parents embrace their children, the family affec-
tions evidently being strong among these good people. It is
not a long business for them to go to bed, as they stretch themselves out on the ground, the women remaining in the same
room as the men, separated only by a sort of awning made of
rough canvas, and stretched on to reeds from the ceiling.

November 7.—It is very cold, and when we get up there are
eight degrees of frost, with a strong north-east wind. Before
leaving we endeavour to get a little sport in the reeds, but they
are too thick, and we cannot go far. Moreover, we are told that
the wild boars, which used to be very abundant here, have been
driven away by a tiger. We should gain nothing, therefore, by
going farther eastward, and if we have any spare time, we prefer to
ascend the Tarim, this side of Abdallah, towards Lob. Our return
journey is accomplished without mishap, though we are overtaken
by a tempest which at once freezes and blinds us, and are
compelled to wrap ourselves up in our *touloupes*, and to pull our
fur caps down over our ears and eyes. Having thus voluntarily
rendered ourselves deaf and blind, we sit quite still at the risk of
getting our feet frozen, so as not to disturb the equilibrium of our
boats. We are not sorry to see Couznetzoff again and the fire
before which he is cooking some birds.

November 8.—One of my first visits is to the cemetery of
Abdallah, which is situated on three sandhills the other side of

the Tarim, its site being indicated by poles on which are placed the heads of horses or the tails of yaks. Upon one of the hillocks. perhaps that reserved for the burial of the chiefs, is a small reed hut divided into two compartments, in each of which is a sort of wooden rack filled with the horns of deer and antelopes, while in front of the hut are more stags' antlers, and antelope heads dried with the skin on them. I bring away a few of these horns, hiding them under my coat, and in the afternoon go off for a ride with Barachdin and a guide who is to show us the way to a large lake to the south-east. As we leave the village we meet a Mongol caravan consisting of about fifty camels and twenty horses, most of them fully loaded, coming from Karashar. The Kalmucks who are riding them are on the way to meet their Sovereign, who, as we learn, has lost most of his beasts of burden on his way from Lhassa. It is useless for us to stop and talk with them, for they would give us no information of any value, so we continue our march. After riding about six miles, we reach two small depressions in the ground which are barely moist, and beyond that there is no vegetation, the stony desert extending to the first spurs of the Altyn Tagh. There is not the slightest trace of the great lake we have been told of, but our guide says it was there three months ago. He adds that half a day farther on, extending his hand towards the south, there are ruins, supposed to be the remains of a large town, nearly buried in the sand, only the tops of the houses being visible.

On our return, we find the village of Abdallah in a state of uproar, the whole population rushing about, shouting and gesticulating; the men saddling their horses in haste, the women and children crying, and two old women, bent double, groaning in quavering tones and exclaiming, "Allah! Allah!" The horses are soon ready, and the men, with Kumshikan Bey at their head, all make off in the same direction. We watch them till they disappear in a cloud of dust, and when we ask the meaning of this, the women, who have calmed down a little since the departure of their husbands, soothed, perhaps, by the consoling tones of the gallant Abdullah, proceed to tell us, still sobbing at intervals, what has happened. They ask us if we do not see something in the direction in which the horsemen have gone, and when we tell them "No, nothing but dust," they say that the men who went off on a shooting expedition a month ago have been seen, but that whereas three started, only two have returned. Two of the three were sons of Kumshikan Bey. In the meanwhile, the little band of sportsmen draws closer, and then it is seen that all three are there, so that the lamentations are turned into rejoicings quite as noisy. The whole village went out to meet the three men, who were on foot, with emaciated faces and clothes much torn, walking very slowly and leading three donkeys. When asked what had become of the two other beasts, they said that they had died of cold, and the loss of these two animals excited fresh lamentations from among the old women.

After the elders who had gone out to meet them had got off their horses and kissed them, the young men were made to get down and tell the story of their adventures. First they went southward and then eastward, and though they had seen a great many wild camels, they had only killed two, the second at six days' march from here. The skins had been cut up into rectangular pieces and loaded on a donkey. Nearly all the hair had been rubbed off, and they had put it into a bag for fear of its being spoilt on the way.

The return of the *chasseurs* * and our presence in the village are made an occasion for amusements in the evening. The women put on their smartest things, in most cases a watered silk dress, reminding one of the Bokhara stuffs, with red in front, while

---

* It seems a pity that we have not in English a comprehensive word, like " chasseur," to designate those who go shooting, hunting, or fishing, as the case may be. Even " the chase " is only used now to designate hunting.—*Note of Translator.*

the wives * of the chief have a caftan trimmed with black sheep-leather, while one of them wears her rings passed through one end of the fichu which she has on her head, having taken them off her fingers for fear of injuring them while cutting reeds for the fire. One of the women is rather pretty : a Khotanese, with regular features and a pale complexion, which brings into relief her big black eyes, surmounted by finely-arched eyebrows. Like her companions, she is short in stature, but, being better looking, she excites their jealousy. Madame Tocaesch, to give her her name, very much regrets her native land, finding Abdallah too savage, and, to mark her disapprobation, she ran away a few days ago to her parents, who reside at Tcharkalik, but they, instead of taking her in, informed her husband, and helped him to get her back. An honest man, when he has sold his daughter and been paid for her, would consider that he had committed a theft if he took her back to the prejudice of his son-in-law, and as to the girl herself, she is not consulted in the matter.

Madame Tocaesch shows her superiority over her companions by the grace with which she dances. She is accompanied in her dance by some of the men, who nod their heads as they move round, and stretch out their arms, which are hidden in the long sleeves of their *kalat* (large cloak). Although they are agile and light-footed, the dance—to which our Russian plays a tune upon his harmonium, two or three of the old women chanting in a nasal tone—soon becomes monotonous.

November 9.—The minimum of temperature is about one degree below zero, but although the morning is cold there is no wind, and it is, therefore, good weather for going up the Tarim. Before leaving Abdallah we make a few final purchases (of snares, dried fish, sandals made of donkey skin), payment being effected in Chinese money, which has to be weighed, a slow and

---

* It must be remembered that we are among Mussulmans, each of whom has at least two wives—they are fairly cheap.

troublesome operation to which we shall have to get accustomed.
Kumshikan Bey and his family allow themselves to be photographed
again, and he gives us a supply of small loaves of bread made by
his wife, and wishes us a safe journey. We promise him to
return "some day," but in the meanwhile we have to make a
start, and choosing between various modes of locomotion, I go on
foot as far as the first Abdallah, where I take a cup of tea (with a
piece of butter in it) with the old centenarian, whose sons are
sharpening their spears and getting their guns ready for the
pursuit of the wild camels. They accompany us as far as our
canoes, which have arrived from the other village of Abdallah,
and, with the weather not so cold as it was yesterday, we ascend
the stream, our boatmen finding it very hard work to row against
the strong current. Floating pieces of ice come into collision
with our canoes, and we are at times almost hemmed in between
them, the oars having no hold upon their surface. In the bends
the river is completely frozen over, and we have to break the ice
and clear a passage, reminding one of polar navigation. The two
natives who are in charge of our big canoe sing all the time,
one having a strong harsh voice and the other a falsetto. We
imitate their singing in order to raise the drooping spirits of our
own men; but in spite of all their efforts they cannot make much
headway, and we have barely advanced ten miles in a straight
line when we have to stop for the night. Our donkeys and horses
have overtaken us, and having picketed them, we roll ourselves
up in our rugs and pass a very pleasant night in the open, despite
there being twenty-seven degrees of frost.

November 10.—Navigation, difficult as it was yesterday, now
becomes impossible, and we have to be content to follow the Tarim
by going along its banks. We meet boatmen whose canoes are
firmly fixed in the ice, and they say they have been in this plight
for three days, unable either to go back or to advance. They ask
us to give them some food, which we do as far as our scanty

means permit, and then resume our journey, coming, a few miles higher up, upon a pile of bags, and of reeds which have been cut and laid out on the banks. This is opposite a small village called Tchaï, the inhabitants of which are about to migrate to Tchar-kalik, and have already taken their luggage across. When they see us making for their bags they take us for thieves, and begin to run away; but when we assure them that we mean them no harm, they gradually gain confidence, and on our offering them a cup of tea they become quite convinced that we are friends, and give us all the information we ask for. They tell us that the sheet of water from which we see the Tarim issue a hundred yards or so above Tchaï is the Kara Bouran, though it is little more than a series of inundations, representing the largest stretch of water to be found in the Lob Nor. It begins at the village of Lob, and ends here, being interspersed at many points with lagoons and islets. It is nowhere more than three feet deep, in most places only a foot, while the lake which we skirted above Lob is the Kemezetiantché, which does not communicate with the Kara Bouran, for since Prjevalsky came into the district the course of the Tarim has been changed, and the level of the water has fallen.

These indications save us the trouble of following the bank of the Kara Bouran, and we determine to make a short cut across the country opposite Tchaï.

While the light still lasts I try for a little shooting on the Kara Bouran; but we have great difficulty in getting the canoe there, as the current of the Tarim is very strong at the entrance to the lake, and when we get there it is a sheet of ice, so we have to give up the idea of going any farther. My excursion, though a brief one, is not altogether fruitless, for I succeed in bringing down with No. 4 shot a very fine white swan of the species which is domesticated with us, as he flies over my head, while with a bullet I kill a goose flying in the midst of a flock, these being two

shots which I should be sorry to back myself to repeat. In the
evening the natives attempt to surprise us by their learning, and
repeat the word " Podi siouda," a Russian term, which they have
retained in their memory since the visit of Prjevalsky.

November 11. — Commencing our march by moonlight, we
observe for the first time the phenomenon which will strike us so
often upon the high lands, viz., a sudden drop of the temperature
as the sun appears above the horizon. We are at present very
insufficiently protected against the cold, and although we are
walking, we shiver from head to foot, while, for my own part, I
do not know what to do with my hands, which are so numbed
that I cannot get them warm. We have no choice but to wait
till the sun has got up, when a fresh trouble arises. We are in
a desert the sand of which is in many places covered with a layer
of salt, and the refraction is so great that we are constantly being
led astray by the mirages, while we are dazzled, blinded, and half-
roasted by the sun into the bargain. It seems as if all the sun's
rays were converging upon us, and as if there were no choice but
to let ourselves be thoroughly baked.

Our horses do not seem to be so much affected by the heat as
we are, and I really believe that they can smell their stable, though
still more than thirty miles off. There is no road, and we have
to guide ourselves by the compass; but the instinct of our horses
is the best guide, and we speed along at such a rate that a courier
sent forward by Bonvalot has scarcely time to hand us a letter.
It arrives rather late, for we are already in the oasis, and before
long we see a rivulet, some gorse, then some tamarisks, several
small poplars,* and, last of all, Rachmed, going off at a great pace
after " those wretched hares." In a few minutes we are in the
camp, which has the aspect of a small town, with people coming
and going in all directions, buying and selling, gossiping, and
nailing down boxes, while in the centre is our little tent, beneath

* *Populus diversifolia.*

which Bonvalot, with his legs crossed Turkish fashion, is enjoy-
ing a meal of sparrows, cooked on a skewer with slices of sheep's
liver in between them.

All is well at Tcharkalik, our Russians are preparing for their
return, and two men of the country have been engaged to
accompany us. The provisions are gradually accumulating;
bread is being baked with
plenty of salt in it, sheep's
paunches are being filled
with fat, the salt is being
purified, and the preparations are well advanced.
Our men, however, have
been greatly obstructed in
their work by a tempest
which lasted two days, blew
down the tent, and covered
everything with sand. M.
Bonvalot has effected a

SPINNING WOMAN AT ABDALLAH.

regular massacre of hares, and we, in return, give him an account
of our excursion, which has lasted a week, and during which
we have traced the course of the Tarim in the Lob Nor, and
have ascertained that this latter name does not now apply to a
lake, but to all the marshy portion of the country watered by
the Tarim, from the village of Lob to the end of the river.

The largest stretch of water in this region is the Kara Bouran,
a tract under water between Lob and Tchaï. The waters of the
Tarim are not salt, while there are springs of fresh water (Eutin)
in the Lob Nor, but the water of the pools formed by the Tarim
upon a saltpetre surface is brackish. Each year the quantity of
water which the Tarim brings into the country decreases, the
pools dry up, and the reeds are more and more covered by
the sand which is gradually driving the inhabitants towards

Tcharkalik, so that the time is not far distant when the region called the Lob Nor will no longer be distinguishable from the desert into the midst of which it now advances like a narrow ribbon of verdure unwinding itself from west to east for a distance of about a hundred and twenty-five miles.

CHAPTER V.

FROM TCHARKALIK TO THE KOUM DAWAN.

"The Southern Road"—Taking Stock—New Recruits: Timour and Iça—Festivities at Tcharkalik—A Nomad Moralist and Poet—Tramps—Prince Henry's Return—Taking a Chief into Custody—The Dungan and His Master—The Start—Yandachkak—The Altyn Tagh—Valley of the Djahan-Saï—Tchouhour Saï—Through a Cañon—Prince Henry Lost.

November 1.—We* are so far from having completed our work that what we have hitherto done has been little more than a simple excursion, attended by drawbacks so trifling that they merely gave an interest to the journey. I have said that the first stage was Kourla, the second is Tcharkalik, and the third would be Batang, if all continues to go as well as at present. Batang is a long way off, separated from us by deserts and the unknown. After Batang we hope to reach Tonquin, at the other end of Asia, but when travelling there is not, fortunately, much time to reflect upon the difficulties before one. In the meantime we have constantly in our minds the passage in the narrative of the English traveller Carey, published in the Proceedings of the Geographical Society of England, in which he speaks of a route going to Lhassa by the Kizil Sou, a river supposed to be beyond the mountain chain which Prjevalsky saw, and which he named Columbus. Carey had heard the natives talk of this route, but they had never shown it to him. According to rumour, it is more direct than that of the Tsaïdam, which joins the route of the Koukou Nor, first travelled by Fathers Huc and Gabet, and afterwards by Prjevalsky.

We must, therefore, at all costs discover this route which, in talking of it, we call "the southern route." We send our men to make inquiries, and each of them endeavours to light upon the

---

* The narrative is here resumed by M. Bonvalot.—*Note of Translator.*

invaluable individual who knows it and is willing to guide us.
But the mere fact of one of them having asked in a stupid sort of
way is sufficient to prevent us from getting any definite information.
Moreover, very few of our men care to pursue the journey. Our
three Siberians are going to leave us. They had agreed to come
as far as the Lob Nor, but I cannot persuade them to come on
farther, and the Dungan camel-driver is also anxious to go back,
being only kept with us by the promise of high pay. So we look
out for volunteers in the district, and two offer their services, one
of them knowing the Bokalik road, which Carey took. We
promise them good wages, and their arrival helps to raise the
spirits of the Dungans.

The chief of our camel-drivers, the aged Imatch, though he
walks with great difficulty, will hold on to the last, and will go
wherever the Khotanlis go. Parpa has already been over the road,
and he does not show the white feather, but he puts on a mys-
terious air which I do not much like when I speak to him of the
southern route. If he is to be believed, he is acquainted with a
very good guide, but does not know his name. He says, however, that he can find him, and begs permission to go and ask for
information in the village, and in the farms scattered about in the
bush. He returns without bringing any important tidings, and I
soon ascertain that he has been after something very different
from the southern route.

As to our interpreter Abdullah, surnamed the "little man,"
he is still a terrible talker, and a busybody who sees that things
are not progressing as he would like. He did not think we were
in earnest when we talked at Kuldja of going to Batang, his
idea being that we should perhaps go as far as Kourla, and then
follow the main imperial road to Pekin, or that, at the outside,
we should go to the Lob Nor and then return. Now he is
beginning to get anxious, and would like to dissuade us from
going farther, so we are convinced that we shall not get

information of any value from him, though he professes to be more or less enthusiastic.

To judge by what we have seen of the two fresh recruits, we shall have reason to be satisfied with them later on. The elder is

called Timour, and has been a shepherd, while he goes in for gold-mining and the chase when he has leisure. He is a married man, and cultivates a small plot of ground, and as he has often explored the Altyn Tagh and the Tchimène Tagh, he feels no hesitation about accompanying us over the high table-lands. He executes orders without any trouble, is a quick worker, and has the reputation of being indefatigable on the march, while he takes good care of the horses and camels. He is always in good spirits, and, this being a very important point, is content with his lot at Tcharkalik. A very small piece of sugar suffices to make him happy, and he seems to take an interest in all we

15

do, for he looks at our arms with manifest pleasure and tells us the names of the birds we have prepared for our collection. In the evening we can hear him singing and telling stories, and when Rachmed or one of the others is relating an anecdote, he follows all the details of it with close attention. In short, he is a poet and an adventurer. When asked if it will be cold in the southern mountains, he says yes, and thrusts his hands under his sleeves and warms them under his armpits. " But," he adds with a laugh, " that will be nothing." Withal he is not too tall nor too stout, is very alert, dances well, knows so many prayers by heart that he is taken for a mollah, and possesses remedies for various complaints.

The other man, who is only about twenty, is called Iça. He is full of vigour, and can skin a sheep very dexterously, and cook rice well. He is equally good at eating both, he takes an interest in all that relates to cooking, and is ready to split wood, light the fire and attend to it, fetch water, and clean out the saucepans. He has a very loud laugh, but so natural that one likes to hear it, especially as he is generally rather stern. He has a good memory, though he is said to be given to smoking haschisch in small quantities, but those whom he has previously served give him a good character. I saw him one night sleeping on a mat before the fire with no covering except a *khalat* torn in several places. He was sleeping very soundly, though the fire had gone out and the minimum temperature of the night was two degrees below zero. As he was very well the next day and had not caught the slightest cold, I did not want to know more.

We renew our provisions, the important thing being to ensure plenty for the subsistence both of men and of beasts, for from all we have read and from all we can learn on the spot, those who have preceded us were obliged to turn back from want of provisions. It is as important to feed the beasts of burden well as the men, for when the means of transport fail all exploring is impossible.

As we can procure flour and barley here and get it made into bread, we employ all the women in the place, one procuring us one hundred pounds, and another fifty pounds, and we make them bake a small quantity at a time, and taste it to see that it is what we want. We buy all the dried fruits we can get, as well as rope, horse-shoes, and nails, while we have winter clothing made for the horses and camels.

The men's pelisses are sewn and made larger, trousers and leggings are made out of sheepskins, and plenty of leather leggings are provided, as well as leather stockings, into which the foot is inserted after it has been well wrapped up in felt. One of our Russians is a shoemaker, and we employ him to make our felt boots, while the men prepare their own according to the fashion of their respective tribes.

There is a regular market every day on the outskirts of our little camp, and what with the chaffering, the disputing, and the laughing, the scene is very animated. We gradually get on friendly terms with the natives, and at the end of a week have acquired a certain degree of authority at Tcharkalik. We have created a " French party " in the place, and it is among the members of this party that we shall find men to transport our provisions for a month or more.

On the birthday festival of Mahomet the authorities came in a body to pay a visit and offer us presents. They were anxious that we should participate in their rejoicings, for we were far from home and hearth, and it would be unbecoming if they were not to invite us. I thanked them, and repeated the assurance that we had no bad intentions in our hearts, affirming that our acts would always be in keeping with our words. They said they believed what we told them, and asked permission to entertain our men. This, of course, I readily granted, and all day long the festival of Mahomet was celebrated by feasts, songs, dances, and sports, in which Rachmed, who is very agile, obtained marked success. Two sheep which we had given them were cooked in the immense pot belonging to the mosque. This pot came to a bad end, as we burst it while using it to refine crystallised salt—a mishap of evil omen which was atoned for by a present.

PARPA.

November 8.—A terrible tempest from the north-east howled all last night, and compels us to construct a shelter for our kitchen. The temperature drops very suddenly, and this morning the natives appear in the guise of North-erners, all of them wearing sheepskins and the furs of wild animals, such as foxes and wolves. Our people avail them-selves of the opportunity to try on their winter costumes, and very odd some of them look.

A man arrived in the course of the morning from Abdallah village with donkeys and horses, bringing at the same time some wild duck, and a letter from Prince Henry. Another piece of news announces the arrival at Abdallah of four Kal-mucks, who are believed to form the advance guard of the Khan of the Kalmucks, this personage being on his way back from a pilgrimage to Lhassa. He is expected to arrive in a very deplor-able condition, as his caravan has been decimated, and he has lost two hundred camels and twenty men. He has made the return journey chiefly with *koutasses* (yaks), and has come by way of the Tsaïdam, for the messenger says that when the Khan of the Kalmucks attempted to reach the "City of the Spirits," some twenty years ago by way of the Kizil Sou, he had to turn back because the mountains were impassable.

The *Aksakal* of the Khotanlis having brought me some marmot fat as a cure for an attack of rheumatism from which I am suffering, I questioned him about the route of the Kizil Sou, and, without giving a definite opinion, he let me understand that little importance was to be attached to what the Lobi says. As regards the difficulty of the route, he says there can be no doubt as to that, and that upon one occasion, when he went in the direction of Bokalik with one hundred and fifty asses to bring back gold and skins, he lost a number of his beasts and some of his companions. Their death was due to the cold, and above all to the pestilential odours emitted from the soil, which were even more fatal to the asses than to the men. It is impossible to learn anything definite as to this route, the existence of which we regard as more than probable. The natives of Lob and Tcharkalik have never followed it, and the Kalmuck pilgrims have no information on the subject. Parpa asserts that a guide whom he knows is returning with the band of the Khan of the Torgots, and he asks leave to go and meet him at Abdallah. This leave I refuse, as he has two months' wages in his pocket, and with the cold weather setting in, he might be tempted to return home.

After the tempest, the atmosphere is more free from dust, and the sky becomes clear. It freezes, however, harder than the natives care about, the minimum under the tent being 10° This sudden fall of temperature has alarmed the population, all of whom have quitted their houses and now make off into the bush, those who are strong enough to do so carrying a faggot on their backs. The Aryk is frozen, and the fields in fallow are white with frost; and the last of the swallows have fled to warmer climes. We, too, are impatient to make a start.

After the storm had raged for two days, the sun reappeared, and, with the sparrows chirruping and the natives returning to our camp, business begins to look up again. For the purchase of the smallest bit of cloth, or a pound of grapes,

interminable speeches are made, and the names of Allah and of
Mahomet his prophet are incessantly invoked.

November 9.—The minimum is 2° below zero, with a refresh-
ing breeze from the north-west, while it is 70° in the sun.
The natives have turned the waters of the Aryk into the wells,
so as to secure a full supply for the winter; and for the
last week the mills have been going, in anticipation of this
time of scarcity, each householder being anxious to have plenty
of flour in store.

A singer, who seems to me very proficient, accompanies
himself upon a guitar, and gives us a song as we sit in front
of the fire; the dancers, male and female, going through their
performances to the same music in more or less graceful attitudes.
The burden of the song is that the world is all delusion, and that
man is always looking for the realization of desires which it would
be as difficult for him to obtain as it would be to seize the moon,
though he sees her every month.

The singer is said to be the author of the couplets he
sings, and we ask him to accompany us in our journey
and bring with him his guitar, which is made of two pieces
of poplar wood; for a moralist like him would be a desirable
acquisition to our party. He has travelled about a good
deal, having been to Yarkand, and prospected for gold in all
sorts of places, but he does not appear to have made his fortune,
and it is his disappointments that have inspired him with this
doleful song. He has the reputation of being an honest fellow,
and at the festival of Mahomet he won the wrestling prize in the
"Olympic" games. Although a native of Khotanli, he is the
intimate friend of a certain Abdullah Ousta, who is very proficient
in the art of iron-working, and who belongs to Lob. Some years
ago Tokta, as the singer is called, did a considerable service to
the aged Abdullah. The latter had got lost while pursuing wild
camels, and would not have been able to rejoin his companions

had not Tokta come upon him when he was almost dead with hunger and fatigue. From that time the two men have been very much attached to each other.

We have ordered some iron nails and pegs from Abdullah Ousta, and we hope to enroll him in our party, for Tokta assures us that there is no one better acquainted with the mountain than the old man, who is still very vigorous, though his beard is white. If he consents to accompany us, his example will be followed by many others.

Tokta, before leaving us, says that we shall get plenty of help if the white beards of the Lobis do not interfere, and that the Khotanlis are all in our favour.

Rachmed says Tokta may very well be trusted, because he is " Saïa."

" What is ' Saïa ' ? "

" A man like ourselves, who cannot stay long in one place, owing to his mother's fault."

" Explain yourself."

" That is what happened in my case, and must have done in that of Tokta. Our mothers, when pregnant with us, travelled through the desert on camels; and as they strained their eyes to see beyond the horizon, they made of us 'Saïa,' or tramps. And that is why we are again about to march southward, and Allah alone knows when and where we shall stop. And we shall do well to start, for the route seems to me a long one, while those cursed camels do not go fast."

Thereupon Rachmed reproaches me for having taken him into my service when he scarcely had any beard, of having made him grow more white hairs than black, and of having made him miss several desirable marriages. Then, being very volatile, he flies off at a tangent and plays some joke upon the man next him, loading him with the insults which the Uzbegs offer in all good humour.

Rachmed is right; it is urgent that we should start, but

all is not yet ready.   The Dungan must make up his mind to go,
and then we can apportion the loads according to the strength of
the different animals.   At least forty donkeys and ten men are
required to relieve our own beasts a little, and feed them, as well
as the men, for a month.   The Khotanlis have as good as promised
us half, but the question is whether the Lobis will supply the
other half.   It is always difficult to be prepared for every con-
tingency when setting out for a long march.   We find this out
once more, and Rachmed confidentially mentions that he has
doubts with regard to the Dungan and the Lobis.

As soon as Prince Henry and Dedeken return from the Lob
we shall settle these questions ; in the meantime the best course
will be to display great amiability, to pay liberally, and never
to refuse a request for medicine or drugs.

November 11.—While busy eating some roast sparrows cooked
by Parpa, I heard the voice of Prince Henry, who arrived in high
spirits after a journey of over forty miles since daybreak.   He
appears to be in excellent health and condition, and his first
question, after inquiring how we all are, was as to when we
were to start.   While I was telling him how we are situated
Father Dedeken arrived, and to celebrate our re-union, we
had tea got ready and a repast cooked.   While it was in preparation we talked of the Lob Nor, and their conclusion is that it
is but a vast marsh interspersed with jungles, amid which are
hidden the dwellings of fishermen.

Before starting we have to arrange for the return of our
three Siberians, as they are to go back to Kuldja with our collections and letters, which the Russian Consul will send on for us
to Paris.   We give them camels for conveying the packages to
Kourla, where they will purchase an *arba* (sort of waggon), for it
is their intention to return by the imperial highway of Urumtsi,
making the circuit of the Tien Shan (Celestial Mountains).   We
give them plenty of food and ammunition, and should have much

liked to retain at least one of the three, but Borodjin was married, and Maltzoff had undertaken the journey so as to make a small sum for her wedding, while the third, Couznetzoff, whom we had engaged at Tiumen, would not have been as useful to us as

AT THE FOOT OF THE ALTYN TAGH.

either of the others, for he is no longer young, and is unfitted for very severe labour; but as an assistant in our naturalist work, he has always been most conscientious and willing, display-ing care, order, and patience. We cannot be too thankful to him or say too much in his favour.

November 12.—We ask the municipality to supply us, at a price to be mutually agreed upon, with horses, and with donkeys to carry a portion of our provisions as far as the vicinity of the Kizil Sou, by way of the Bokalik route. We are promised an answer for to-morrow, after a council has been held.

November 13.—This morning we see a large body of men approaching our camp ; the chiefs and nearly all the people of the

16

village, Khotanlis and Lobis alike, being present. They halt at the threshold of our temporary domain, and a tall fellow with a scanty goatee, whom we have not seen before, opens the conversation, and explains himself to Rachmed, who interprets what he says. We learn that the speaker is the principal chief of the Lobis, and he says in so many words that they will give us neither men nor asses, because it is too cold for mountaineering, and that to travel over the table-land at this season is certain death, etc.

Rachmed, in very gentle terms, insists. He reminds his hearers "of the good we have done in the country, of the money we have spent in it, of the high prices we have paid for everything with the object of being of service to the poor vendors;" then he asks how it is that the promises made to us but yesterday are not kept, and inquires whether we have given reason for supposing that we shall not pay, as we have promised to do.

In the meanwhile we learn that secret orders have arrived from Kourla. The Lobi chiefs are said to have been prohibited from rendering us any assistance, and as they have asked for the aid of the Chinese against the Khotanlis, they are determined to obey orders and to put obstacles in our way.

The Lobi chief gets arrogant, and exclaims, "By Jupiter! if you want donkeys you shall pay twice their value, and I won't sell you any. As to men for your service, not one shall leave the country. We are not under any bond to you; we do not pay you a tax—we pay it to the Chinese. No, we are under no bond to you, and we are not afraid of you! We have numbers on our side, we are brave, you cannot frighten us!"

As he spoke, Rachmed, who felt the necessity of immediate action, used the *argumentum ad hominem*, and began to belabour this great orator. His own people were inclined to defend him, but we drove them back by threatening them with our weapons, and kept the leader in custody, stating that we would only release him in exchange for the eighteen donkeys and five horses, which constituted the contingent the Lobis were to supply. The Kho-tanlis then intervened and acted as mediators between the two parties, interceding for the chief, who was very downcast, and promising that they would make things all right.

We hear the exclamations of the women upon the roofs and in the brushwood, the dogs bark, the donkeys bray, and there is a general uproar.

However, the chief whom we had in our clutches was con-soled with a cup of well-sugared tea. Timour advised him to think better of his decision, as he had everything to gain by obeying us, and as we were certain not to give him his liberty again until we had made sure of his co-operation.

The chief then asked for one of his men, and ordered him to "give them what they ask for." This messenger returned to the assembly which was being held some distance off, in front of the palace of a chief who has a wife belonging to Lob, though he is a native of Khotan. Some emissaries were at once sent back to us to ask that the king might be set at liberty. But we refused this unless certain guarantees were given us. The messengers returned, and a fresh council was held, with the result that they came back in a body, accompanied by the grey-beards, who swore that we should have as many donkeys, guides, and hunters as we desired, but they were not to go further than the land of the Kalmucks of the Tsaïdam.

They add: "We cannot show you the donkeys, because there has not been time to collect them, but here are the Lobis who will accompany you." The men are then made to step forward, and we are asked to examine them. Then follow declarations "by the beard" and "by Jupiter," and all the divinities are invoked; the crowd approves, gesticulates, and lifts up its voice, while all around us are people smiling, waving their arms with suppliant gestures, grinning amicably, and murmuring assent to whatever any of the others may say.

It is only at the last extremity that we agree to let the chief have his liberty, when the crowd and the chiefs who inhabit Tcharkalik have authorised us, by their beards, to indulge in reprisals if they fail in their promise to supply us with what we require. They instruct one of their men, who offered us hospitality on our arrival, and with whom we have always been on friendly terms, to organise the contingent. Our host assents with a nod, while the other chiefs inform us that they are going to be absent for several days, their duty being to go and meet the Khan of the Kalmucks on his way back from Lhassa.

The principal chief, having been set at liberty, soon comes to take leave of us, and, with his nose slightly swollen, repeats the promises already made, and swears that he has given orders for them to be executed. After a profuse display of politeness, he mounts his horse and. rides off. Our camp relapses into comparative silence, the crowd having dispersed, but we hear on all sides fresh exclamations and positive lamentations. What can have happened? Upon inquiry we find that all the noise is being made by the women whose beasts have been requisitioned, and who are moaning and groaning to each other on the roofs over the sad fate of their jackasses.

We are not dissatisfied with the day's work; the submission of the Lobis has led to that of the Dungan camel-driver, who obstinately declined to go any further, despite the engagement he had entered into, and a treaty signed with his thumb, or rather to which he had applied his thumb smeared in ink. But although the Dungan resigns himself to his fate, it is not without heaping maledictions upon those who have acted as interpreters. He keeps on exclaiming, " I have been put into a bag," and vents his ill-humour upon his servant Niaz, who is a native of Tourfan. And as Niaz has not been paid his wages, he retorts by asking for what is owing to him, and even for a little on account, as he is not clad warmly enough to encounter severe cold. But his master is sordidly mean, and, as Niaz says, is the worst-tempered person in China. We have to interfere on his behalf, whereupon the Dungan takes the opportunity of asking for an advance from us, for he says he has to settle his accounts and send money to Kourla. Niaz tells us not to believe a word of this, and says his master will not pay his debts, but will hoard up his money.

November 15.—All these little things indicate that it is high time to be off, so we finish our preparations, writing letters, and paying the men who are going back, as well as those who are coming with us, and others who have supplied us with provisions. We have added to our caravan three dogs of the country, two of which are enormous hounds of the kind here called *pista*, forty donkeys, and a dozen men in two detachments, one under the orders of Abdullah Ousta, the other commanded by Tokta, the Khotanli. We have, I think, taken every conceivable precaution against the unknown, for we have with us two canoes and paddles in case of our being brought to a standstill by a river, and if we do not want them for the water, we may be glad of them as fuel.

November 16.—All is ready. We take with us 700 small bundles of hay to feed our horses, which are bound to die off the first. We have taken into account the probability, not to say the certainty, of deaths, in order to fix the quantity of rations we need to take with us, and it is in proportion to the number of beasts of burden that we have ; so that the load may decrease as the animals die, and that the survivors may not be over-burdened just when their strength has declined. Experience tells us about how much is wanted to feed the fourteen men of our regular army for five, or, at the outside, six months.

The sight of these bags and chests imparts courage to Rachmed, who exclaims : " With the help of Allah, all will be well."

Yet, if we are to believe the natives, we shall not go far, for they say that the camels will not be able to cross the Altyn Tagh if they follow the route taken by the Englishman Carey, while the "little man" will have it that Prjevalsky was of the same opinion. However, we are impatient to put the matter to the test, and the start is fixed for the 17th.

November 17.—In the morning the animals were loaded, amid a scene of great excitement, the whole population being present— women, children, friends and relatives of those who are going with us. It was not merely the sight of our departure which attracted them, for they had come for the same reason as the sparrows, which, perched on the willows near the camp, were only waiting for our departure to swoop down upon the grains of barley on the ground, just as the crowd of onlookers was eager to seize the empty boxes and bits of cloth which we were leaving behind.

At last the caravan is ready, and we start, amid bright sunshine, accompanied by the chiefs on horseback, who will go with us to the camp, a few miles from Tcharkalik, the first stage being always a very short one. It terminates at the entrance to the desert, on the other bank of the small stream which makes the oasis, and from which we shall once again get good water. To us, who have drunk so much brackish water, this is the most delicious of liquids.

Forty minutes on horseback suffice to take us out of the oasis into the desert, and as we get out of the saddle to sit upon the felt where the chiefs offer us "the stirrup cup," we cast a glance towards the Gobi, with its deceptive mirage of beautiful lakes, the mountains to the south-east just emerging out of the mist.

Before sunset, the elders bid us farewell, the beaten chief, who is not the least cordial among them, being of the number. To him, as to the others, we offer a present, and they say, as they wish us a successful journey—"May Allah grant you good

health, and take you back safe and sound to your families who
are so far off! We are poor, and have not been able to do as
much for you as we could have wished. You will excuse us.
May Allah protect you!"

We shook hands with them and thanked them, regretting
there should have been a little misunderstanding, but they had
never seen any men of our race, and were suspicious. We expressed a hope that they would henceforth receive any of our
countrymen with open arms, and would not retain an unpleasant
recollection of us, but regard us as friends. Then they exchanged
confidences with the goldseekers and trappers who had determined to go with us, and who said, "Look after my father; urge
my wife to be patient in my absence. Give her corn on credit; I
will pay when I come back. Take care of yourself. May Allah
keep you," etc. Then they embraced one another, those of the
same family kissing lip to lip, while others squeezed the hand of
their seniors, who imprinted a kiss upon their foreheads. Next
a grey-beard recited a prayer, and when he had done, they all
raised their hands to their beards and exclaimed, "Allah is great!"

The wife of Timour, a small and very active brunette, has
remained with her husband. She is very quick at sewing bags,
while her son, a little boy of four, clad in sheepskin, with a dirty
face, snub nose, and the small and piercing black eyes of his father,
amuses himself by tapping the boxes, and singing "There is
only one Allah," until, at sunset, our three Russians make up
their minds to part from their companions. After an exchange
of embraces and good wishes, they return to our camp of the
morning, where they have left their luggage. We hope that the
letters they have taken will get to Europe in about three months,
and we go to sleep after having gossiped about the future, being
all agreed that so far we have succeeded wonderfully well.

November 18.—The minimum temperature of the night was
only 16 degrees of frost, but this was sufficient to freeze the

river, and we take some ice out of it. We shall not get any drinkable water at the place where we encamp to-night, and in future these lumps of ice will be our only drink.

We are in the bare and stony desert; to our right being a dark and indistinct mass looming out of the mist, which the aged Abdullah says is the Altyn Tagh, the gold mountains which have not before been visible in our approach to them. They appear to be lofty, but none of their details can be distinguished, and no peak is discernible. On the other side, he tells us, begins the land of ice, and we shall find it very cold.

Our troop is rather silent, and the men, instead of chatting cheerfully as is their wont, flick their horses in a mechanical sort of way, with a fixed look on their faces. The morrow of separation is always melancholy, especially when one is bound for the unknown, and neither physically nor morally is one up to the mark.

We approach some sand-hills on our left, the outposts of the Gobi. It is there that we are to encamp, our donkeys and the flock of sheep we take with us for food on the road following us very closely, and making a pretty picture as they are driven along by men wearing white frieze. From the sand we get on to *takirs* formed of fire-clay, and then again on to the sand, going up and down hillocks formed by the crumbling away of the mountain and the sweepings of the plain.

Abdullah Ousta, getting off his horse, begins to search for water, which he is not long in discovering, from its proximity to the salt on the surface; and when the donkeys have been unloaded, the men take their pickaxes and dig a hole, which is soon filled with salt water.

We make some tea, which we drink pending the arrival of the camels with the ice; and though it is not very nice, we must apprentice ourselves to the desert. I have often noticed that whenever one starts on a long expedition there are some cases of

TCHOUKOUR SAÏ (*p.* 133).

illness in the caravan, and to-day four or five men declare that they are quite done up, though the stage was a very short one and we have been favoured with beautiful weather. This is what one may call desert sickness, similar to the discomfort experienced by some sailors for the first few days they are at sea.

This place, called Yandachkak, abounds with *ioulgoun* (tamarisks), and our brilliantly illuminated encampment reminds me of one in the Oust Ourt, where there was an abundance of *saxaoul.* In the evening we have no fewer than four fires going at once. Our men might perhaps be more economical of their fuel, but the thought that, further on, they will not be able to get any, makes them anxious to make the most of the opportunity, and there is nothing more cheerful than the flames of a bright fire lighting up the gloom of the desert.

After supper Abdullah Ousta, accompanied by some of the men, comes to talk to us and to ask if we are still determined to follow the " old road," as that taken by Carey is called. He points out that we shall be brought to a stop by two passes, and he repeats that Carey, with donkeys, had the greatest difficulty in passing them, as Parpa would tell us. The first is called the "Sand Pass," and one reaches the foot of it by so narrow a gorge that very probably the camels would not be able to traverse it. Moreover, there is no sort of track over the Sand Pass. The second is called the " Pass of Stones," and its name indicates that it is very dangerous to camels' feet. His conclusion is that we should follow the " road of the Kalmucks "— that is to say, the Tsaïdam route—which is the best, while by the old road we should be five days without water.

While thanking him for his observations, we repeat that we intend to follow the " old road," our conviction being that this is the branch of the southern route which we are intent on finding, and we add that nothing will induce us to change our minds till we get proof to the contrary. The men withdraw after promising to serve us faithfully and obey us implicitly, and we send them a little tea and sugar, which they drink while seated around the cheerful fires. The air is filled with melody, which proceeds from Tokta, our poet, who is scraping his *allahrabób*, and, with a pure voice, is singing a very plaintive song, which strikes one as charming in this environment. The song seems to be inspired by the sand, by the cavity out of which the brackish water is drawn, and by the sterility of the soil. It is the song of one who confesses to being overcome by nature—the plaint of a captive asking if he can ever escape from the forbidding solitude in which he is enveloped.

November 19.—At break of day, we hear that the camels are missing. Men start off in search of them in all directions, and it is not long before they are led back through the desert.

The route is monotonous and stony, and the higher we get the larger become the stones, which trappers have piled up at short intervals so as to mark off the road.

At last, the Altyn Tagh is visible to our right, its slopes appearing devoid of all vegetation, eaten into as they have been by the waters; and the eye can follow the burrows in which the shadows wind along, deeper or shallower according as they denote the course of the streams, the torrents, or the rivulets, by which the water drains off the mountain.

Having marched for six hours nearly due east, we halt in a valley watered by the Djahan Saï, which also bears the name of Kuntchi Khan, a great Lob chief. He is said to have come from the Tsaïdam with his flocks, and, having discovered this river while on a hunting expedition, it took his fancy and he brought his family to settle here. This river is said always to have plenty of water, which we can quite believe, as its whitish, milky colour indicates that it proceeds from a glacier. The natives say, indeed, that there is a small glacier at its source. The volume of water is considerable, but the sands suck it all up before it reaches the Lob. About ten miles to the north of our camp, half-way to Abdullah, the land is irrigated and cultivated, and after the harvest is gathered, the tillers of the soil go to live in various villages near Lake Lob.

These indications as to a discovery made by a chief coming from the Tsaïdam render it probable that the natives of Thibet must have become intermixed with the Lobis, though not in any great measure, a supposition to a certain extent confirmed by the fact that, when we had penetrated into the centre of Thibet, we heard the natives singing the same melodies as the people of the Lob Nor.

The valley of the Djahan Saï is characterised by blocks of granite which have been scored, perforated, and fashioned by nature, and which affect the shape of boughs, bones, shoulder-blades, and shafts of columns, the aspect being that of a cemetery, the tombs of which have been profaned, and the corpses hacked to pieces and scattered to the winds.

We come upon traces of gazelles and also of donkeys, and are told that some *chasseurs* from the Lob have recently returned with the remains of *koulans*, a species of horse which roams in large troops over the highlands.

November 20.—In the morning the level of the river had risen a little. Its water is still white in colour, and Abdullah Ousta is confident that at a week's march south-east there is a glacier.

We encamp at Tchoukour Saï, and on the way come across some *saxaouls*, from which our men at once make faggots, being well aware that there is no wood in this district which emits more heat. These shrubs still bear their berries, but unfortunately these are unfit for food.

Our camp is in the desert, beyond the Tchoukour Saï—a deep gorge without one drop of water. We shall halt a day here, and send our animals to feed on the mountain, near to some water, as it is indispensable to undertake the passage of the

Koum Dawan and the Tash Dawan with beasts which are fresh.

November 21.—To-day is accordingly devoted to rest, after a night during which the temperature was only about five degrees below freezing, with a light breeze from the north-west, while in the daytime the thermometer rose to fifty degrees. We spend the day in effecting various repairs and in cleaning, everybody being in good-humour, except the Dungan camel-driver, who has set up his bivouac a little way from ours, and is sulking. His attendant Niaz says he is in a viler humour than ever, and that he keeps on grumbling and declaring he has been humbugged. Niaz adds that he is like a dog being led along with a string round his neck, showing his teeth all the time, and he is, therefore, glad to come to the fire with our men, being always sure they will give him a drink of tea.

November 22.—Three-quarters of an hour from the camp, after the first, but not the last, pass of this journey, we descend more than 100 yards into a cañon, which shapes its way southward, and comes out at the foot of the Koum Dawan. This cañon is very picturesque seen from above; it narrows as one gets higher, while immediately below us it is a narrow gorge, in which the water has left numerous deposits. From all sides the high and steep banks have caused the sand to silt down, and there are frequent lodgments of the alluvium, in the mass of which large cavities have been eaten out.

Advancing in this defile, we reached a narrow gallery paved with ice, lying under the mountain, which the water has eaten into. It would not require a great effort of the imagination to fancy oneself in an enchanted palace. But if the entrance to this gallery was easy, it was more difficult to get out of it. We had to climb up steps formed by enormous stones which had rolled down from above, and which the camels could not get over After having examined the route further on, and concluded that it was practicable for these awkward animals, we determined to clear a way for them at any cost. With their iron pick-axes, our men succeeded in two hours' time in making the passage feasible; and, having got the camels through, we bent a little to the south-east, and en-camped beside a stream not yet frozen over. The water, though a trifle salt, is quite drinkable, and we should be very thankful never to taste worse.

In this region there are plenty of traces of wild animals, such as wolves, foxes, and gazelles. A troop of fine animals with curved horns looks down upon us from the crest of the hill as we get off our horses, and it is evident, from the foot-prints on the banks of the stream, that they were coming down to drink. Our appearance has brought them to a standstill,

THE DUNGAN.

and when Prince Henry fires a shot at them, the whole troop scuttles off at a tremendous pace to the opposite side of the gorge. Prince Henry goes in pursuit, and when night sets in he is still absent. So we go off in search of him, for fear of some accident having occurred, and discover him, not far from the camp, upon a rocky ledge, from which he can neither come down nor go back. At last, by means of ropes, we get him down, and he returns to the camp very well satisfied at having made the acquaintance of the *koukou-iaman* (*Pseudo Ovis burhell*), but disappointed not to have found the one he had wounded.

Thus it is that we form acquaintance with the fauna peculiar to Thibet. The incident shows how quickly travel binds people together, for our men, though they had had a hard day, did not need any telling to go in search of Prince Henry, being sincerely anxious about him, and ready to start in a moment.

I thank them, as they sit round the fire, for their energy, and it is a good sign that they do not indulge in too many pro-testations, their silence indicating that they have no thoughts to conceal. Seeing, close to our camp, traces of men and donkeys, we question Abdullah Ousta on the subject, and he tells us that a month ago a party of fourteen men, including two of his sons, went on a shooting expedition in the direction of Bokalik. When we ask him if the Kizil Sou is in that direction, he says it is, but that he has never been there.

It is clear that whenever one speaks of the Kizil Sou, it is impossible to get any information, and I notice that Abdullah Ousta appears to be ill at ease, while the others, who say nothing, could give us some information, if I am not mistaken. So I say—

"Has no one been to the Kizil Sou? Yet it is said that there is a great deal of gold to be found there. Don't you know anyone, Abdullah, who has lived in those parts?"

"There is not one of us who has been to the Kizil Sou. But I may say that a man of Lob is there at the present moment. He left the Lob last year, and we have no news of him."

"What was his object in going?"

"To seek for gold, though he took arms with him for shoot-ing, so that he might be able to supply himself with food, the country being uninhabited."

"Is he alone?"

"Yes, he has not even a donkey with him. He is a poor man, beset by creditors, to whom, not having the means to pay them, he gave his only son in pledge, and as his son works for his principal creditor, the father, having resolved to procure

CAÑON AT THE FOOT OF THE KOUM DAWAN (*p.* 134).

his son's freedom, asked permission to go off on this expedition. He made his own powder, got some shot given him, took his pelisse and his tools, and set out for the region where gold is found. He begged his neighbours to give themselves no further concern about him, as he did not intend to return till he had secured a sum sufficient to pay his debts·and make him free of creditors for the rest of his life. He went off at the beginning of last year, and we have heard nothing of him since."

It is difficult to say whether this story, which has quite a Biblical flavour, is true, or whether it has been invented by Abdullah Ousta, in order to show us that he is anxious to keep us well informed; for there is no reading the hearts of these Orientals. However, we must keep our weather eye open.

CHAPTER VI.

STRIKING THE SOUTHERN ROUTE.

Ascent of the Koum Dawan—The Beginning of Mountain Sickness—A Musical Evening—
At Uzun Tchor—Iça's Reformation—A Caravan Sighted—The Plain of Tchimène—A
Providential Meeting—Bagh Tokai—The Southern Route Discovered at Last—Making
for Namtso—Diplomacy.

November 23.—From Boulak Bachi—that is to say, the " Head
of the Spring "—we made our way towards the first pass, which
we had been led to expect with so much apprehension. After half
an hour's march along the side of the gorge, we descended into the
dry bed of a torrent, and halted at the foot of a sand mountain.
This is the Koum Dawan, which has to be climbed, and as it is
devoid of the slightest vestige of a path, to us falls the doubtful
honour of tracing one as best we can. It is useless to think of
ascending the course of the torrent with our camels, and of
following the donkeys, which, after they have been unloaded,
are hoisted up the steep path as if they were themselves so much
baggage. There is nothing for it but to attack the Koum
Dawan. Our troop sets to work and endeavours to make some
sort of a route for the camels by use of the feet, the pickaxe, the
spade, etc., care being taken to render the ascent gradual. Then
the file of camels is set in motion. The sand is extremely fine,
and does not, on the slope, offer sufficient resistance for the
camels to find a place where they can with safety put down the
large hoofs of their clumsy feet. They keep falling on to their
knees, and as this is their resting posture, they remain quite
content and bar the passage to those behind. Our men have
great trouble in getting them up, and in some cases they keep
dragging themselves along on their knees till they are flogged on
to their feet. It is a long business to get them over, and it
is accompanied by quite an orgie of imprecations and curses,

the word *our*, which means "flog," being the most frequent. The heavily loaded donkeys and the sheep bring up the rear, with drooping heads and ears.

After a repetition of the same incidents, and after having crossed two sandy ridges, we descended by a steep path into the same valley which we had quitted in the morning. The ascent of the Koum Dawan had taken us eight hours, and although we had only got a few hundred yards higher than the camp of the previous day, our men complained of violent pains in the head, accompanied by cold feet. This was the beginning of mountain sickness, and old Imatch was the principal sufferer, for he was weak on the legs, and as he had to get off his horse and walk he was quite exhausted.

AKOUN.

November 24.—We made our encampment not far from the Tash Dawan. The nearer we get to the mountain, the more deserted does it seem. It is quite bare, and in all directions narrow ridges emerge out of the dust and sand. Mountain sickness continues to prevail, and this is beginning to be so alarming in its proportions that it will be a relief to have crossed the Tash Dawan, or "Pass of Stones," which, as we are assured, is more difficult than the "Sand Pass."

November 26.—To-day and yesterday have been devoted to the Tash Dawan, our troop being quite exhausted. Several of them have been bleeding from the nose, though we have not yet reached the altitude of Mont Blanc. The ascent is so steep that we have been compelled at times to hoist up the camels, and men have had to carry the baggage from the bottom. We are encamped in the midst of a narrow stony valley, quite arid, and without any sign of brushwood. Our provision of ice is diminishing, and the animals have not drunk for two days. So the new recruits who find themselves in this desolate mountain are quite out of heart, and full of gloomy forebodings. The Dungan in particular is very exasperated, and keeps on saying, "If the route is not better further on, what is to become of us? And there is very little chance of its improving, for from the summit of this accursed spot we can only see in front of us mountain piled upon mountain." When little Abdullah goes up to the camel-driver and salutes him politely in the hope of getting some of his Chinese delicacies, he is greeted with an outburst of insults and curses, the Dungan shaking his fist at him, spitting at him, and calling out with angry sobs, "Cursed dog, you have deceived me; you come to contemplate your work. You want to see whether I am near to dying. Be off with you!"

Little Abdullah makes off at his best pace, and I am disappointed at not being able to eat any of this Chinese paste; for, cut up small, cooked in water and with fat, and well seasoned with salt and pepper, it makes a rather agreeable article of food, in default of anything better.

The night was a particularly bad one, for Rachmed, who had been after megalo-partridges, did not return till very late, and when the anxiety which this had excited was alleviated, the men were kept awake for a long time by mountain sickness. We could hear them moving about and sitting up to relieve the oppression on the chest, while others vomited, and there was a long succession of groans and complaints, the pass being treated to plenty of curses in Chinese and Turkish.

Fortunately, Abdullah Ousta promises them that the next encampment shall be close to a river, with brushwood and even a little grass, so that they may regain their strength, with which their courage also will return.

November 27.—We start with a north-west wind, which makes the 23° of frost very hard to endure, and at night the minimum was just below zero. More than one of our men has to breathe on to his hands while handling the ropes, or even a compass or the photographic apparatus. But we begin to descend, and the mountain sickness decreases, the men feeling their heads steadier on their shoulders, and the singing in the ears being less accentuated. The difference in altitude of a few hundred yards suffices to restore those who have been amiss, and when we are protected from the wind between the sides of the ravine a sensation of relief is experienced.

After five hours' march we arrived by the small pass of the Obo (Dawan Island), on the banks of the Djahan Sai, the sides of which have a fringe of ice, though in the middle of the stream the water flows along rapid, clear, and drinkable.

We had traversed hillocks of sand and of soil where the camels found it no difficult matter to plant their feet. One might imagine that there is in this region a reserve of vegetable soil destined to cover the unfertile surfaces of our planet with a stratum of the black earth in which food-giving grain does so well.

The traces of animal life are frequent just here, the large hoof of the *koulan* being seen in many places near the river, as well as the forked foot of the *arkar*, while several *koukou-iamans* had been by the site of our camp a few minutes before our arrival. The camels go along with their eyes fixed on the ground; now and again they inspect the mountain and its rocks. Abdullah declares that we are about to come upon abundance of game, and when asked about the route, he says that further on the stones are not so frequent, and that the ground is nearly everywhere soft. We take care not to speak to him of the Kizil

Sou and the southern route, as we must make it our business to discover it for ourselves.

December 28.—While the evening meal is being cooked, the saddles and clothes are cleaned, and Rachmed makes a ramrod out of the branch of a tree. Parpa sews his boots, made of wild-camel skin, with antelope tendons, which he softens by dipping them in his teacup. The horses and camels are allowed to roam about, and the dogs snarl and fight over the sheep's entrails.

A sumptuous feast is being got ready. The rice is washed for the *palao* which will follow the *caverdak*, this dish, which comes first, consisting of bits fried in mutton-fat. The *caverdak* is not allowed to simmer long in the pot, and it is eaten while only half-cooked. Little Abdullah, who has not the patience to wait for the *palao*, obtains, by dint of entreaties, a shoulder out of which only part of the bone has been taken, and toasts it before the fire, tearing at it with his teeth and fingers, and exclaiming, "Here is a foretaste of Thibet and its fare." A light is thrown on to the pot by means of the branch of a tree which has been rubbed with mutton-fat to make it answer as a torch. The repast being ready, the Khotanlis join our men, and there is quite a family party round the boxes which keep off the north-west wind. No one fails to do justice to the banquet, and Rachmed sarcastically observes that we shall not run short of warriors to fight battles of this kind. The fire lights up the tanned countenances and white teeth of the men as they dip their hands into the bowls and scoop up pieces of rice, which they jerk into their mouths. They eat till they are full, and the fragments, which are very considerable, are taken to the Lobis by the youngest; the arrival of the cooking pot, still half-full, bringing a smile of contentment to the faces of these savages. We all appreciate the agreeable character of this evening, which obliterates the recollection of the fatigues and disappointments of the previous days. We even have some music, Tokta having brought with him his instrument—his *Allah-rabób*, as he calls it. This is because the *rabób*, having only three strings, cannot be compared to the great *rabób* of India; it only serves to play

IN THE CAMP AT OUZOUN TCHOR.

simple pieces, such as invocations to Allah, whence the *Allah-rabób*. The Dungan, whom the prospect of watering his camels has made amiable, keeps open house, and offers his Chinese dough all round. Although the men have barely finished a copious repast, some of them accept the offer, and seem none the worse for this second meal when they return to the camp fire and go off to sleep. Most of them sleep without undressing, merely lifting their arms out of the wide sleeves of their pelisse. The Lobis undress and sleep quite naked, curled up among their clothes, wherein they double themselves up, after having first warmed them in front of the fire to dry them and to drive away the

19

vermin. They do not shelter themselves from the wind behind
their bundles, but behind the fires, so that the wind blows the
heat of the flame on to them. This is the best plan when in the
open air.

December 3.—We have reached Ouzoun Tchor (the great salt-
pit) by way of Pashalik, Kara Shote, and Mandalik. These names
do not signify that we met any habitations or human beings, for
we have passed through an undulating desert, with a north-west
wind blowing up a great deal of dust. We have followed pretty
closely the route taken by Carey, but without finding any water at
points where he, in the month of May, had seen rivulets running,
whereas we have had to carry bags of ice with us. We intend to
halt near the great salt-pit, for we want some salt. Yesterday we
had a strong hurricane from the north-west, with twenty-seven
degrees of frost. The minimum of the night was sixteen degrees
below zero; so that there can be no mistake about winter being
upon us. In the morning the wind falls, and the sun comes out
in full splendour, the temperature rising to fifty-nine degrees,
though in the shade it is four degrees below zero. (Time,
9 a.m.)

While the men were off to shoot, I went to see what I could
discover, with my eyes never off the ground. To the south of our
camp rises a very bare, deeply-scored, and crumbling mountain,
the slopes of which slip away as the foot, sinking into the sand,
rests upon the surface, breaking away like sugar. This mountain is shedding its sand into the plain and gradually driving
back the vegetation, while in the large basin to the east spreads
the vast yellowish-green surface of the Ouzoun Tchor, marbled
with streaks of salt. In the more remote distance, between the
east and the south, a small lake glitters, reflecting the hills which
overshadow it, and close to its shores are some *koulans* browsing,
though they soon make off in great alarm. Beyond the basin in
which the salt-pit is situated a steppe rises gradually towards

other mountains, the summits of which are hidden in the mist. This chain diminishes in altitude northward, and seems to be connected with other jagged mountains which close the horizon to the west.

On getting back to the camp, I found that Prince Henry had killed a fine male *koulan*, this being his first, and that two men had gone off to cut up the beast and bring back his skin, with a little of the flesh.

December 4.—The night minimum has been 20° below zero, but the north-west breeze is, fortunately, very slight. We had to wait until the sun had got the cold out of our men, and had melted the frozen ropes, before we could prepare for a start. While we were drinking our tea Timour made an exclamation, and when I brought my glass to bear in the direction of the brushwood where I was yesterday, I could clearly distinguish two or three donkeys and some men armed with guns. All at once they disappeared, and then, as a thin column of smoke curled up into the air, we saw that they were halting to cook their food.

We at once sent Abdullah, who supposed them to be Lobis, to talk with them, but we let Rachmed follow him at once, so that he might not set the new comers against us, and prevent us from obtaining information. Soon afterwards four men came to our camp, the two oldest offering as presents three foxes' skins and one wolf skin. They were somewhat intimidated by our presence, though our men crowded round them and pressed their hands, inviting them to come near the fire. But they did not venture to cross their legs, and were evidently very ill at ease.

These men are veritable savages; their clothing, which is of frieze or sheepskin, is all in tatters, their faces are sunken and their bodies wasted by privations and long marches, while their hands look like veritable claws. They are small and thick-set, with the physiognomy of Turco-Mongolians, and they might be taken for Turkomans, with their long noses and thick nostrils, their prominent cheek-bones, and small brown eyes.

We treat them hospitably, and give them cooked meat, tea, bread, and sugar. They put away the meat, drink the tea, and scarcely touch the sugar, after they have just licked it. But they break the bread with great care, and eat it solemnly, as if it was food which would do honour to their bodies. Gradually their figures expand, and they seem to be well content. One of them, whom we have christened "the Tzigane," on account of his bushy black beard, leans over to his neighbour and mumbles a word with a smile. They exchange a look which can only be interpreted into surprise at being so kindly treated. Whether they think well of us for our reception of them, or are inclined to despise us for our weakness, it is impossible to say; for in the desert men are not disposed to be very tender to one another, and first communications are rarely of a friendly character.

These savages are, perhaps, stupefied at the good nature of the strangers, who, being better armed and stronger than themselves, treat them kindly, offer them a good price for their skins, and promise them some food for their journey to the Lob Nor, when it would have been so easy to despoil them. So we take advantage of their being well disposed to question them.

"Have you seen the son of your friend Abdullah Ousta?" we ask.

"Yes," replies one; "he has not found much gold, but he is shooting. He is in good health."

"Have you seen any traces of wild camels?"

"No, though we know that they roam at times through this region."

"Do you know the roads?"

"Abdullah knows them better than we do; he is a grey beard."

"You have not seen any Kalmucks?"

"No, not one. They live beyond the Tchimene Tagh, which is the frontier we have mutually agreed upon. We do not go beyond it on our shooting expeditions."

It is impossible to extract any further information from them, and we begin to think that they have nothing to keep back, and so we thank them, and our men give them many commissions for Tcharkalik. Tokta sends a message to his little boy, and Timour to his wife, whom he exhorts to be patient and not to desert his home. Iça, who sends a message to the son of his master, the *Aksakal*, has the bad habit of smoking haschisch, and Rachmed had accordingly nicknamed him Bangi (which means smoker of haschisch). This annoyed him so much that he came to complain to me, but I reasoned with him and got him to see that he deserved the appellation. So I advised him not to smoke any more, and then he would be treated as a good Mussulman, and I would make him a present. One fine morning he had broken his haschisch pipe, and as he had a little *bang* left in his bag, he availed himself of the visit of these men to send it to his friends, with the following message:—"You will do well not to smoke any more *bang*, but if you do, smoke this which Iça sends you, and pray to Allah that our journey may be successful."

Thereupon the men went off, and after Rachmed had regretted not giving them a bigger piece of sugar, the tents were quickly struck, and in an hour and a quarter we reached the extremity of the Ouzoun Tchor, which is not frozen over, and on the banks of which is a thick layer of salt. We wound round the end of the lake, following a rather narrow slope near the mountain, leading to a defile which is called the "Neck of the Ouzoun Tchor" (*Ouzoun Tchornin Boïni*). Here we came upon traces of camels, but whether wild or domesticated it is impossible to say. As we were riding quickly on, exclamations arose: "Look, there are camels!" "No! yaks, I tell you." And, sure

enough, about five miles to the east was a caravan with animals
bearing loads and accompanied by horsemen. We concluded
from the steady and regular march that this was a caravan of
camels, and at once ordered Abdullah and Akoun, our Chinaman, to overtake the travellers, whom we presumed to be
pilgrims in the suite of the Khan of the Torgots, who had
recently gone through the Lob Nor. As they were trying to catch
up the pilgrims we entered the defile of the Ouzoun Tchor, which
narrows as one gets higher up. The caravan had just been
through it, and the footprints left by their camels prove that
camels can go a long way. We also found traces of the Lobi
chasseurs, and the examination of the soil caused us to lose a little
time and enabled our Lobis to get ahead of us. They had not
followed the route of the pilgrims, whose traces were along a very
easy path, through the hills to the right of the defile.

Our inclination was first of all to make the advance guard turn
back and to take this new route. But Abdullah Ousta dissuaded
us, declaring that the route was very bad. We did not believe
him, but followed his advice, pending the return of the two men
we had sent on ahead, knowing that it would not be difficult for
us to find the road again.

The defile terminates in a pass, from which we descended by a
plateau called Tchimène, this being the beginning of the chain
of that name, of which we catch a glimpse to the south in the mist.
We trotted along an excellent road over a bare sandy tableland,
then descending towards the plain of Tchimène along some
spurs of hills. Suddenly two men, mounted on camels, appeared
from behind a ridge just within range of our glasses. They were
evidently frightened at the sight of us, for they set off at a slow
trot, which is a dangerous pace for beasts on high ground. Our
idea was that these travellers were rejoining the caravan which we
had seen, and Dedeken, who speaks a little Mongolian, set out in
their pursuit at full speed. He caught them up, and questioned

them, and returned quickly to tell us what he had gathered. They were two Torgots belonging, as we thought, to the caravan, on their way back from Thibet, where they had been to worship the Lama at Lhassa. As they were short of meat, they had gone off in search of game, and had killed a yak, which they then cut up, carrying off the best pieces for their comrades—and it was these quarters of meat which we had seen swaying as they hung from their saddle-bows. They had asked Dedeken where we were going, and he had prudently replied that our intention was to go hunting eastwards, in the direction of Se-tchouen. These various meetings supply food for thought, and give us the hope that we have hit, if not our ideal road to the south, at all events a good one, for here are pilgrims who have followed it on camels— camels, too, which are still capable of trotting. Farther on there must be inhabitants, for these hunters told Dedeken that within half a day's march live some Kalmucks.

These uplands form a glorious picture, but at the bottom of the pass, on the right, Timour points out to us three stones supporting a pole which is planted on the spot where lies the body of one who, when out hunting, had died on the road. A barely perceptible path to the lowly tomb has been made by the feet of the few Mussulmians who go there to pray for one of their comrades.

From the eastward direction which Abdullah Ousta makes us follow, it is evident that he means to take us to Tchong-iar, and thence to the Tsaïdam. To-morrow we will modify our line of route.

We camp on a sort of terrace in the midst of some scrub and brushwood, and the night being dark, and our camels not having arrived, we set fire to a thicket, and the flames bursting forth show our whereabouts as a lighthouse does the harbour. Abdullah and our Chinamen, the last to arrive, told us they had counted twenty-one camels carrying chests protected by skins.

They recognised these camels as belonging to the Kalmuck race; and they had evidently too, come a considerable distance, for they were lean, and their harness was much worn, while the covering of their loads bore signs of bad weather. Their feet, however, were neither cracked nor barked excessively, so it was plain that the road had not been a stony one. The only rider in the caravan was a veiled man, a lama with a grey moustache, who deigned to speak to them from the back of his camel, though unwilling to give them any information. He assured them that he was coming back from the Tsaïdam, from a place called Timourlik, and was on his way to Abdallah. He would not acknowledge that he was from Thibet, but asked them point blank, " Are you in the service of the Russians ? "

" No," they answered.

" We know that some Russians are anxious to penetrate as far as Lhassa, but they have not received permission to do so. If you are these Russians, don't forget that."

" We are in the service of some Frenchmen who have not the least desire to enter Thibet."

" What have they come here to do ? "

" Hunt."

At this reply the lama lowered his veil and said not another word. His servants gave out that he was " a living Buddha."

We summoned the hunters of Lob and Tcharkalik, and asked whether they know the road which this caravan had followed. After much pressure, we wrung an avowal from old Abdullah Ousta. " Twenty-five years ago," he said, " I heard that some Kalmucks had returned from Thibet by a more direct and easier road than that from the Tsaïdam. That's all I know."

Thereupon the old hunter asked permission for himself and his men to leave us. " The cold," he says, " is becoming more and more unendurable, daily our homes are farther off, and

IN THE TASH DAWAN.

provisions are diminishing." I promised an answer next morning, but this very night Rachmed informed him that we would let them go as soon as we had recovered the track of the caravan, and that they should be richly rewarded, for we were very well satisfied with them. We thus secured their assistance in hitting upon the right track.

They replied that they were happy to have met us, and their old chief swore that all would serve us faithfully to their last breath. Up to a late hour they kept up a whispered conversation round their fires. In spite of all their loud protestations I know they would desert us at the very first opportunity, but we can very well do without them.

This 4th of December will be a white-letter day in our travels. What a coincidence! Just at the decisive moment, just at the spot where the road separates, we have providentially met some pilgrims on their way back from Lhassa. It is too fortunate, and we must make the best of so valuable a piece of information. To-morrow we will again track the two yak hunters, and see where their traces lead.

December 5.—We set out in a south-westerly direction, leaving the Tsaïdam on our left. Towards the east the vast plain, wrapped in what looks like smoke, attracts our attention. At first we imagine there must be an encampment there, but this vapour unfolds in spirals just as the smoke does from the engine of a train, and we conclude that a herd of wild beasts is galloping over the soft ground. We are in a kind of dusty plain; after walking for five hours we enter a river-bed where a torrent has brought down some roots and branches, which we carefully collect. They will serve to melt the ice which we have brought with us, for since the 20th of November we have had no water and have no idea when we shall get any; we are short, too, of grass.

December 6.—We continue our south-westerly course, eager to

arrive at the foot of the hills towards which lead the tracks of
the pilgrim hunters, and we ask Abdullah Ousta if he knows the
next encampment. He says he knows it by hearsay, and that
it is good; it is called Bagh Tokai, which means " Garden of
Brushwood."

When we approach Bagh Tokai, we find that the name of
garden is not too grand a one. We are near a fresh-water
river, as we gather from some bits of ice that sparkle in the dry
bed of one of its affluents. The stream, on reaching the low
grounds of the plain, has left behind it some large pools, frozen
of course, and formed an endless number of arms; at the edge of
the channel we can see the water running. The Kalmucks have
camped here, and we soon see the prints of their camels on the
ridges which they have scaled so as to avoid the ice on the river,
while in the brushwood which here forms a thick plantation, we
easily recognise the spot where they lit their fires. Besides
these very recent traces, there are others much older, which
Abdullah Ousta says are those of the Khan of the Kalmucks,
who went to Lhassa by this road before the frost had set in, for
the feet of the laden camels had sunk deeply into the soft ground,
and then the frost preserved intact the traces of the first passage
of the caravan.

At night we hold a council of war, questioning our hunters
and our friends, and insisting that they undoubtedly knew the
place already. Old Abdullah denies that he has ever set foot at
Bagh Tokai; but, driven to extremities, and as the result, perhaps,
of a talk with Timour, he tells us that the latter can give us
some information, since he knows much more about it. The old
hunter is unwilling to unsay his words, for fear he should be
punished for his untruthfulness, but, to pacify us, he has charged
Timour to tell us about the place. So the latter begins:—
" Parpa can tell you, as well as I can, that we are now on
the road to the pass of Amban Ashkan, for he has been

here with two Europeans.* I believe that there is, beyond that pass, a road into Thibet. This is how I discovered it just eleven years ago." (Rachmed pours Timour out a cup of tea, and hands him a lump of sugar.) "It was the year that Badoulet (Yakoob-Beg) was poisoned by those cursed Chinamen. I was hereabouts with some bold companions, on our way to Bokalik to seek for gold, when we came across a caravan returning from Lhassa, consisting of Kalmucks who were accompanying the mother of the present khan. They had camels and yaks. After following their road back as far as Amban Ashkan Dawan we saw with our own eyes that their tracks led southwards. That is how we found out this route, which the Kalmucks keep secret, for they only speak of that of the Tsaïdam."

I have no idea of reproaching Timour, for I am too pleased.

"Does this road go to the south, once you have crossed the Amban Ashkan Dawan? Answer frankly, Timour."

"Yes, it does; straight to the south. At least, the tracks disappeared in that direction."

Decidedly we have hit the southern route so long sought for. The only thing now is not to lose it.

Our original idea was to go to Tonquin *viâ* Batang, crossing the Tsaïdam, if we could strike the road which, we had been told, starts from Kizil Sou. And now circumstances have dispensed with the need of our seeking the Kizil Sou route. A caravan has gone and returned by the same road, and we will follow its track, and with due attention have every chance of recovering the trail, which must open out near Lhassa, towards which we will proceed as far as we can. Our beasts of burden are in good condition; we have provisions for four or five months more, plenty of ammunition, and men in good health, so that there is very little imprudence in making the venture. If circumstances only prove favourable, we have every chance of success, and why

* Carey and Dalgleish.

should we not go on with what we have so well begun? Such are the ideas that flit quickly through my mind, and prompt me to inform my comrades that we are going to spur due south so as to arrive at the Namtso, the "Heavenly Lake," near Lhassa. We shall certainly make some interesting discoveries, and once there, can think of Batang and Tonquin.

My companion, Prince Henry of Orleans, knew or guessed that for some time I had been thinking of Thibet. Though we had never said anything precise on the subject, I felt that we should have no trouble about agreeing, and when I now tell him my thoughts, he becomes enthusiastic, and replies, " You will see we shall succeed, I am sure of it, and let us set out at once. You can rely upon me. What a grand idea! I was certain you meant going to Thibet." Then I turned to Father Dedeken, who was coming up with his rifle over his shoulder. I had never mentioned to him the projects which I had in my mind, and he was now much surprised to hear them, for we shall not approach the direction in which he at first thought we were going, so he raised certain objections :—" We have no papers. What shall we do? How are we to get out of the hands of the people of Thibet, who act under the direction of the Chinese ? "

" Once there we shall see what to do," I replied. " But we are not yet in their hands."

After a moment's reflection he said, " I will go where you like, at once."

I called Rachmed, who came to our tent in which we were all three having our tea, and having knelt down, as is his wont, near the entrance, asked the news.

" We are going southward," said I. " We shall follow the traces of the Kalmucks as long as they are distinguishable, and if we lose them through our own fault, we will each wear, for the rest of our natural lives, a fool's cap. What do you think of my idea ? "

"Master," he replied, "you are never happy unless you are seeking fresh roads. Though it was of China that you spoke to me before we set out, I knew it was of Thibet that you were thinking. Now all we have to do is to keep our eyes well open, and spare our animals. We shall get out of the difficulty all right."

We next took into our confidence little Abdullah, who was by no means cheered by the news, though he did not dare to make any objection. As to the brave Tundja, also surnamed Akoun, Dedeken's Chinaman, he maliciously remarked that he was well acquainted with the cardinal points, and knew we were not marching towards Urumtsi, nor yet towards Sinin-Fou, as we had promised him at first, but he would follow his master.

I thereupon urged our three faithful followers not to noise our conversation abroad, and to try and persuade the four Dungans and the men of Tcharkalik that we meant to go hunting towards the south, with the firm intention, once the hunt is over, of making our way eastwards, that is to say, in the direction of Bokalik, the gold district.

Before we retire for the night, Abdullah Ousta's men come to inform us that they cannot go any farther; that twice already they have wanted to return, but we had prevented them; that now they really wish to leave us, for they are unacquainted with the road to the Amban Ashkan Dawan. We reply that Parpa, the man who has been with Carey and Dalgleish, and Timour, the goldseeker, will serve us as guides, and that they themselves are perfectly capable of retracing their own steps. Then we promise them a handsome reward if they will consent to transport our baggage as far as the other end of the pass, while, at the same time, we guarantee them payment of a very different kind in case of their refusal. They consent accordingly to accompany us so far, on my promising faithfully not to drag them on any farther.

As to the Dungan camel-driver, he is far from being pleased to learn that we are not going to make for the Tsaïdam, while his servant, honest Niaz, comes to our men's tent in a disconsolate mood, complaining bitterly of his master, and exclaiming—"What a wicked, wicked man ! For the last fortnight

AT BAGH TOKAI (*p.* 156).

he has been just bearable, but since yesterday evening his bad temper has again shown itself. He is constantly swearing at me, covering me with insults, while he reproaches me for the bread I eat. This morning he loaded his own ass, but so badly that to-night the animal has a sore on its back, and then he goes on at me for it, as if I had not enough to do in looking after his camels ! And all because we are going southward, as if it were my fault." And Niaz sighed. " Ah ! " he went on ; " he says that he wants to be off, to return to Tcharkalik and abandon his camels. Allah grant that he may ! I will gladly stop with you, and I won't even claim the wages which he promised me, though he has never paid me more than a quarter of them."

Niaz begged Dedeken and Abdullah to go to the ill-tempered Dungan, who invited them to partake of a little dough, evidently with the intention of questioning them. Niaz followed them as they went, but very slowly, and muttering to himself, " Is it my fault that we are going south ? "

Dedeken soon returned, and amused us by the account of his interview with the Dungan. The latter received them with unheard-of politeness, had offered them cakes, obsequiously handed them chop-sticks, and with every appearance of the keenest interest had asked after their health. Then, the meal over, he asked them, " Where are we going now ? "

" We don't know," replied Dedeken.

"Ah ! ah ! " growled the Dungan in his boots. " Ah ! ah ! I really cannot understand your answer in the very least. How can I believe that 'great men,' men who are learned, know how to read, write, consult books, examine stars, have no idea where they are going ? Ah ! ah ! Who could make anything out of what you say ? Is it true that you do not know where we are going ? "

" We know nothing about it."

" The new year is approaching. Shall we be in any decent place so as to keep it properly ? "

" Doubtless," interrupted the candid Niaz, who had failed to grasp his master's idea ; " we shall doubtless be at some spot, for are we not always somewhere ? "

When Dedeken and Abdullah had gone, the Dungan invited our Chinaman to his table, and renewed his questions— " Where are we going ? " he asked.

" Towards Europe," replied Akoun, who has no love for him. " Don't you see that we are making straight for it ? "

The Dungan, unable to solve the riddle, sobbed bitterly.

21

"They have nonplussed us completely," he said; "all that remains for me to do is to pray to Allah to spare my life. What are they going to do southwards? What astonishing ideas these Europeans have!" To give vent to his wrath, he abuses Niaz: "Idiot, cur! you don't even know how to saddle a donkey. You don't deserve to eat my meal. What did you put that cup here for? And what is that cord doing there? And those saddles, who put them away? . . ."

And Niaz, as soon as he can, makes his escape to our men, repeating, "I am lost. There is his old temper coming out again."

CHAPTER VII.

A DEATH IN THE CARAVAN.

At Moula Kourghan—More Mountain Sickness—A Chinaman's Logic—Crossing the Amban Ashkan Dawan—The Lake which does not Freeze—A Parting: "Forward to the Highlands!"—The Caravan on Ice—Inquisitive *Koulans*—*Orongo* Antelopes: their Strength and Courage—Camp de la Miséricorde—Niaz Sick Unto Death—Timour Missing—His Return—Remedy for Mountain Sickness—Rachmed Lost and Found—Naming a Volcano —Chinese Heartlessness — Death and Burial of Niaz—Another Volcano named — A Hurricane—Keeping the New Year.

December 7.—To-day, without encountering any difficulty, we crossed the frozen pools formed by the river, which appears to descend from the south-east; then we traversed a dusty plain as far as Balgoun Louk, where we encamped in the brush. The stage was a short one, about seven miles, and we take advantage of a fine day to make ready a *koulan* skin, and to repair all the things which stand in need of mending. We have ice within reach, and as we are told that there is no brushwood farther on, we prepare a *palao* for the last time, and several fires are lighted. In future, our only fuel will be the droppings of the yaks.

December 8.—We have come through the desert to Moula Kourghan, which is the name of a ferry over the river. Beyond this ferry the mountains open out a little; and to the south-east is visible a group composed of two peaks connected by a ridge, hollow in the centre, whence the name of Moula Kourghan, which our men translate by "The Camel's Abandoned Saddle." Before the evening mist closed in the horizon, we could see to the south the depression in the chain of mountains which, as we are told, indicates the road to Amban Ashkan Dawan.

From the top of the hill which I have climbed, partly for the view, partly in pursuit of some small hares which have an excellent flavour, I can see our caravan on its way. Presently it takes shelter from the north-west wind in a sort of ravine. The beasts are unloaded, and the bales laid out in a trice, while the camels, the horses, and the donkeys go off in quest of a mouthful of grass. The sheep are sent away in the care of a watchman, for fear of the wolves.

December 9.—We encamp upon the northern slope of the pass, which we reached by an easy ascent, though much incommoded by a south-westerly wind.

Not far from our camp is a path going west, which is said to be that of the gold-seekers, and we are told that it would not take more than ten or twelve days to reach Tcherchène, and that, about half-way, there is a branch road towards Kia. This route is well known to the Khotanlis; and Timour, who has been along it before, says it is a good one, passing up and down hills, the soil of which is soft to the tread. Timour, who admits that he once spent several days beyond the pass, but without penetrating into the mountains of the south, adds: " This route is often used, as in the land of Khotan the custom is to pay the tax in gold; the Chinese confer upon the mountaineers of the extreme frontier the privilege of working the gold mines, which they know exist in the neighbourhood of Bokalik, but they exact a tribute, payable in gold dust or nuggets. This is paid either once a month, or once a year, and that is why the peoples of the districts of Kia and Tcherchène are in the habit of going in search of gold."

Traces of the Kalmucks are clearly visible in a ravine, but they can scarcely be detected upon the frozen ground, and it is necessary to keep our eyes wide open if we are not to lose their track. We notice that in several cases their caravans have been broken up into sections, but for what reason we cannot discover.

We have plenty to shoot at to-day, there being enough game to provide sport for a whole army of sportsmen. First of all, on the slope of the mountain, there is a large herd of *arkars*, browsing under the watchful eye of some magnificent male animals of that species. Then there are some *koulans*, with their quiet, not to say stupid look; while partridges are calling to one another in the gorges; and hares, sitting behind stones, leap off alarmed by our dogs, or sit in their forms and let themselves be killed.

ENCAMPMENT AT MOULA KOURGHAN.

They trust to the colour of their fur, which confounds itself with that of the soil; or, perhaps it should rather be said, they are accustomed to immunity from the men who visit these parts, and their acquaintance with Europeans is made by means of powder and shot. The *koulans* are wilder, and as to the *arkars*, they make off at once.

But if the sportsman has reasons for rejoicing, he has also cause for annoyance, for the altitude reminds him at each step that he is mortal, and that it is idle to hurry, this being the exclusive privilege of the game he seeks to kill. He can only succeed by ruse, for he must glide along, stop and take breath. The least hurry accelerates the action of his heart, and when he puts his gun up he finds it impossible to take straight aim. We have not yet seen any wild yaks, and when we are told that three or four of these animals are quietly feeding not far from the camp, the sporting members of our party hurry off, the expedition terminating in a roar of laughter when it is found that these are tame yaks, with rings through their noses, which the Kalmucks have left behind. They had encamped on a terrace above the spot where we are, and from the number of fires and the heaps of droppings, we conclude that the caravan we met could only have been a fraction of a large band of pilgrims.

Mountain sickness is still prevalent, and several of our men complain of it. This return of headache and singing of the ears may be attributed to the south-west wind which has been blowing during the day. Nothing is more fatiguing than the wind in one's face, when one has to open the mouth in climbing the hills.

Old Abdullah has killed a splendid *koulan* with one bullet from his little gun, and has brought back the skin and several pieces of flesh. But he is tired and has pains in his head, to relieve which he makes an incision in the middle of the forehead, just at the roots of the hair, and his companion bleeds him with the point of a knife. He does the same by his companion, and both of them declare that they are all the better for it. This is the remedy which the Lob shooting and hunting men employ against mountain sickness. A few days ago, Abdullah had a pain in the palm of the hand, and he cured this by rubbing it with the eye of a sheep mixed with fat, and by binding it up in this as a plaster during two or three days. Several of our men have had carbuncles, caused by the action of the cold upon sores made in handling the ropes, one curing himself by a plaster made out of the skin of a centipede. Portions of animals' bodies are often used in this region as remedies, and this is not astonishing, seeing that simples are scarce and that animals abound.

While on this subject, let me give an instance of what logic can effect in the narrow brain of a Chinaman. At Tcharkalik, Akoun, the servant of Father Dedeken, fell ill on the very day that he had for the first time donned a fine cap made of fox-skin, and to measure. He had been seized with violent pains in the head, and an "inflammation of the lymphatic subcutaneous glands of the neck" had been set up. He had not remarked that on the day he had donned this head-dress, of which he was at first very proud, a severe tempest had burst over us, coming from the Lob Nor, and that he had caught cold. Starting with the assumption that his cap, which had kept him warm, had made him ill, he had concluded that the cold would do him good, and so he travelled, in the worst of weather, with nothing but a thin cap on his head. The result, as may be supposed, was that the mischief increased, the inflammation soon spreading to the cheek and the ear. As soon as I saw what was the matter, I advised him to wrap up his head, and finding that he did not do so—the obstinacy and pride of a Chinaman being immeasurable— I told him that he would get a good flogging if he did not take proper care of himself, and handed him over to the care of Rachmed. The latter pushed the fur cap well over his ears, and applied to the swollen place a plaster composed of pieces of mutton fat fried in the pan and covered with some chopped onion, which had also been put into the pan. In five or six days the swelling went down, the Chinaman began to eat, his headache disappeared, and he soon got well, despite the fatigues of the march, and the cold and wind. His confidence in Rachmed was, for the future, unlimited.

December 11.—The passage of the Amban Ashkan Dawan was effected without much difficulty. The ascent is not so very steep, the point at which it terminates being marked by an *obo*. Hares and partridges abound, but there is no sign of big game. From time to time we perceive ice in the gorges, and thin lines of salt run down the sides where before the water trickled.

Beyond the *obo*, the eye ranges over a vast open space shut in by mountains which are lost in the mist. The descent is easy, and the effect of a mirage causes us to see in the plain at our feet islands with the outlines of stalactites. After some time we can distinguish fragments of ice and mirrors of salt, which have produced this illusion, and on making a bend, we see in the south-west a lake, which glitters so that one cannot tell whether its surface is ice or water. Prjevalsky named it the "lake which does not freeze." The southern slope of the pass is the more picturesque of the two, the northern one having the uniformity of the steppe, whereas here the mountain is lacerated by torrents, which have eaten out ravines, accumulated large stones, and so formed deltas and enlarged the route we are following. The chain of mountains winds along in the same direction as the valley, its ridges bristling with ragged rocks and its sides streaked with dark furrows, the blocks of porphyry contrasting with the dark background of sandstone.

Down in the bottom, our path lies over a long stretch of sand, and we forget the landscape for a moment in our search for traces of the Mongols which the wind and the storms have effaced. None the less, we lift up our eyes to look at the strange shapes of the mountain where it trends down to the plain, the crumbling sandstone shaping out into forms resembling those of animated beings and monsters of Chinese art, with gaping grinning mouths.

We pitch our camp on the banks of a river, and right on the track of the Mongols, which we had re-discovered on the plain of salt. There is very little grass, and a complete absence of brushwood, with a wind blowing off the lake, so we should be better off elsewhere. But the traces of the Mongols are very distinct, extending straight to the south, and this is all we think of.

Before emerging from the pass, Timour points out to us the Bokalik route, leading straight eastward.

When we turn in, there is a bitterly cold wind from the west.

December 12.—The wind is still blowing, the minimum temperature of the night having been 18° below zero. Our people appear to be rather sleepy, and not in the best of spirits. The men are crouching and bent back upon themselves, wrapped up in their sheepskins and with their backs set against the wind. I have to shake them up a bit or they would fall into a state of lethargy; and their attitudes indicate that they have had pretty well enough of it. The Lobis alone are at all active, and they are getting ready to return. The others are pensive, and are evidently saying to one another that this is bad sort of weather for penetrating into the mountains without guides. The Dungan, while mumbling prayers, calculates that he would be much better off at Kourla, and inwardly curses the Europeans who act like madmen and not with the good sense of the Chinese. Little Abdullah, it is clear, would much prefer being seated before the fire at Djarkent amusing himself by cracking pistachio nuts on a stone. Parpa has a gloomy look, and Timour and Iça, our two best men, are thoughtful and undecided. Rachmed, old Imatch, and the obstinate Akoun, are the only ones who wear their everyday look. The others avoid looking me straight in the face; and even the Lobis are ill at ease, for they are afraid we shall not keep our promise and let them go after we have got over the pass.

It is necessary to allot work to each man, for we are going to halt to-day, so one is transformed into a tailor, another into a saddler, a third into a shoemaker. The Lobis are told that they will be free to start to-morrow. They will be paid

22

this evening, but they must go up into the mountain and fetch us a last supply of brushwood.

We make every possible effort to retain a friend of Timour— Tokta, the musician—but his younger brother entreats him, with tears in his eyes, not to accompany us, and Tokta is not at a loss for good reasons: "My father is very old, he is quite infirm, he is alone in the house with the youngest of his children. One of his sons came to help them, but the community drove him away because he came from Tcherchène, where there is an epidemic of smallpox. If I am not back soon, it may happen that our family will be expelled and our land seized. My presence is indispensable."

We are sorry not to be able to keep Tokta, for he is a courageous fellow, of exceptional vigour, indefatigable, and always cheerful. I have known for the last two days that his mind was made up, for, before beginning to climb the pass, he hid away his musical instrument carefully wrapped up, so as to pick it up on his return. If he had had the slightest intention of accompanying us he would not have parted from his inseparable *Allah-râbob*. To the best of our ability we recompensed this faithful follower, and in the evening paid the Lobi loaders and donkey-drivers, and purchased from them what little leather they possessed. We made them presents, and handed them letters for Europe and packages containing the collections we had made since leaving Tcharkalik. They promised to hand over these to the *Aksakal* of the Russian subjects at Kourla, who would send them on to the Consul at Kuldja.—Let me add that these worthy fellows kept their word, and that not a single article entrusted to them was lost, the whole arriving safely in Paris.

Timour and Iça, having been questioned apart, promised to accompany us. Besides, they had given Parpa their word to follow him wherever he goes. Parpa also came to speak to us about his father. "He, like the father of Tokta, is incapable of looking after things alone, of seeing to our horses and donkeys. One of my brothers is with him, but he is an incorrigible gambler. I am afraid my father will run short of the necessaries of life before I return, as I can see that we have a long journey before us." He asks us for a rather large sum, which we advance without making any comment, and he says he shall hand the money to Abdullah Ousta.

So the day passes, and at night-time there is a good deal of stir in the camp, the men holding confabulations with one another in an undertone. Rachmed comes to me in the tent and says he believes they intend making off in a body. I tell him not to go to sleep, but to watch Parpa if necessary, and to call me. I shall sleep with one eye open.

December 13.—At daybreak I was astir, and learned that Rachmed had had to threaten Parpa. He had reminded him of the promise he made to accompany us until we allowed him to return. Rachmed told him that his services were more necessary than ever, that he was well paid, and that he could see by the presents made to the Lobis that it was to his interest to serve us well. Then Rachmed added that if he made off we should pursue him, and that we were quick enough on our legs to overtake him and shoot him. Rachmed repeated that if he served us well he would be handsomely rewarded, and Parpa, upon reflection, decided to follow us.

I avoided intervening in the matter, and treated the men as if nothing had happened, distributing a few articles of confectionery and other objects, which they gave to the Lobis for their families. Small pocket mirrors were much appreciated, but these were only given to men who had specially distinguished themselves.

We commence loading rather late, although it is our intention to make a long march, it being important to isolate the men who are in an undecided state. The Lobis and the men of Tcharkalik who are about to return lend a helping hand to their comrades, strapping up the loads, bringing together the camels and saddling the horses—doing all they can, in short, before leaving them.

When all is ready they sit round in a circle, the Lobis pouring out the tea themselves and handing round the cups; then they get up, and our men load Abdullah Ousta with small packages, and charge him to give them to father, brother, wife, friend, or master, as the case may be. Then they stand motionless, old Abdullah recites a prayer, and they all exclaim, " Allah is great! " lifting their hands to their beards as they do so. They kiss one another with tears in their eyes, and Timour commits his wife to the care of Tokta, who is to bid her " have patience, not leave the house, or go and live with someone else. I will come back with money for her "—a discourse which might have been addressed to Penelope.

" Allah is great ! " exclaims Timour once more, and the others repeat it in chorus with him. They go down on their knees to us, and we shake them by the hand and thank them, begging them to retain kindly recollections of us. They wish us a safe journey, and commit us to the care of Allah. They are all of them more or less affected, and if the tears in the eyes of some of them do not trickle down, it is only because the cold congeals them. And so we part, our cry being " Forward to the highlands ! " But we none the less advance slowly, and Prince Henry, Father Dedeken, and myself bring up the rear to guard against possible desertions.

First of all we walk on to the river, making for a hole in the ice which we have made with our hatchets. As we water our animals one after the other, which takes a good deal of time, we can see our companions disappearing through the pass, which presents, towards the east, a striking aspect with its succession of ridges.

At a little distance from the improvised well in the ice, we see upon the banks the skeletons of camels which have been gnawed bare by the wolves. A little farther on we find emerging from the ice the almost intact humps of camels, and upon closer examination we see that part of a caravan has been drowned here, including the camel-driver, one of whose arms is raised as if in an attitude of menace or of entreaty. Beasts and man had been drowned one after the other, and this must

CAMELS ON THE ICE.

have happened only a short time ago, when the ice was not thick enough to bear them. We have nothing of the kind to fear, for the minimum of the night was 18° below zero. Let me add that the Kalmucks whom we met averted their gaze from the victims and passed over to the right.

To-day begins the business of searching for the track, and how long it will last we cannot possibly tell. For my own part, I am afraid that as we get farther on we shall encounter real difficulties, for the wind beyond the Altyn Tagh often blows with great violence, and now that the Columbus Mountains (as Prjevalsky named them) have been crossed, it is easy to see,

by the aspect of the soil, and by the dust which obscures the
horizon, that the wind will do all it can to make us lose our way,
the traces of the road being already effaced where it is not
sheltered.

This first stage is very monotonous, for there is nothing but
the salt and the desert, with a view of plains of *tikène*. One or
two *koulans* watch us from a distance; the east wind is slight,
but piercingly cold, and our men tramp along with their heads
down, regretting, no doubt, the past, and most certainly looking
forward with dread to the future. Then, as we quit the plain,
there appears a plateau at the base of which are enormous waves
of sand moving eastward. Turning round, the chain of mountains
beyond the glittering lake is barely visible, and it is with
difficulty that we can make out the peaks enveloped in mist.
Advancing southward, we make a considerable descent, following
the dried-up bed of a river, going first up and then down, with
the horizon bounded by the ridges of grey hills. Like a flock
of birds lost upon the waters, our band marches along without
energy and without spirit. Is it because we no longer see the
Columbus Mountains behind us, or because, owing to lack of
light, the heavens weigh down upon us, crushing us, and isolating
us from the rest of nature? or is it the result of the separation
effected this morning?

We encamp in a basin, as much as possible protected from
the wind, and the men go off in different directions in search of
roots and *argol*. The latter is very rare, but the *tiskène*, the
kampir, and the *iabshan* suffice for us. These are the Turkish
names of the tiny plants which creep along these inhospitable
heights, and which incessant winds twist about and flatten.

It was quite dark when the caravan reassembled. Rachmed
had been told off to form the rear-guard when Prince Henry
and myself took the lead to show the way. Here and there the
traces were easy to find, but sometimes they vanished altogether,

so this first evening was not a cheerful one, and our men, tired out by a stage which I had intentionally made a long one, went to sleep without exchanging a word. The night was very bright, the wind having dropped and the cold being very severe.

December 13.—The air is very pure to-day, and we can distinctly see the Columbus chain. The Amban Ashkan pass is just to the north of our camp, while to the south-east the Prjevalsky chain rears its snowy summits; and almost due south two peaks of ice some distance apart are connected, as it were, by a snowy dais of dazzling whiteness. Mountains, great and small, surround us.

The air is calm, and we have no difficulty in loading the beasts, but no sooner are we on the march than the wind begins to blow from the west, and the atmosphere at once gets thick with dust, preventing us from seeing any distance or from thinking about anything else. We are compelled to march along, keeping our eyes on the ground, right and left, for any traces of the Kalmucks, our road being on an undulating plateau, rising in a westerly direction, where it is bounded by a chain of sandhills. The traces lead off in several directions, near a valley, within which is a frozen pool, and our caravan goes southwards, halting in a depression of the soil, near a small stretch of ice just to the south of the Amban Ashkan Dawan.

Prince Henry and Father Dedeken have killed a fine yak, which they had to follow a long way, although he had several bullets in him. In future we shall have to shoot as little as possible, for there is nothing more fatiguing than the pursuit of game at such an altitude (14,700 feet). We are at the outset of our exploring, and no one is entitled to be intent upon anything but the discovery of the route; he has no right to tire his horse, to display his energy, to exhaust his strength, or to take a step which does not contribute towards the success of the enterprise. This is a point upon which we all agree, while discussing the

NIAZ.

events of the day, and my companions have no difficulty in persuading themselves that the art of travelling may be defined, very paradoxically, yet very accurately, as "the art of resting."

December 14.—The night has been a bright one, with no wind, and a minimum of 13° below zero. This morning, the sky was overcast, and we tacked about so as to avoid the ravines and encamp on the other side of the plateau, at the source of a river which is now frozen over. We pitched our tent where the Kalmuck pilgrims had theirs, and lighted our fires with the *argol* of their yaks.

The river runs down between high banks westward, and the edges of the plateau we are leaving behind us are eaten away by the waters which invade it when the snow melts. All around us is grass of the late autumn, which seems green and delicious, and which our animals munch with evident satisfaction; while the salt testifies to the presence of water during the rainy season. On the summit of the hills we can distinguish the forms of wild animals, but at too great a distance to tell what they are.

We again observe that the pilgrims have left traces indicating that they do not travel in a single caravan, but meet at certain points, as was the case near the pass of Amban Ashkan and again to-day near this river. This custom may be explained in more ways than one. Some say—and this may be the case—that the pilgrims, not wishing to disclose the secret of this route, go intentionally in sections, so as not to trace any durable path which could serve as a guide to strangers. Others assert that they proceed by *aouls* or tribes, because they have good guides and are not afraid of losing their way, and because by travelling in separate groups they can feed their animals better.

From our camp we can see the path which the pilgrims followed, winding up along the hill which shuts off the route to the south, and curiosity impels me to climb this path and find out what awaits us to-morrow. Once on the top of the ridge, I see again the two large white peaks, which are reached by a green surface, dotted here and there with sheets of ice on the bottoms, with hills all around. Judging by what we have seen up to the present, this is a spectacle we shall often have before us. The Mongolian route appears to take a south-westerly course, so as to strike, to the right of the white ridges, an easier way.

Below me, well out of shot, is a herd of *koulans*, and they do not see me until I am within 650 yards of them, when three males look in my direction. As I stand still, they become reassured and go on feeding. In this way I get to within 400 yards of them, but then the alarm is given, and the troop forms up, with the males at its head. But instead of bolting off, they advance towards me, and as I retreat they come on in a sort of semicircle, actuated, apparently, by curiosity. Can it be that they have a vague recollection of having once lived on good terms with man, and that they would like to renew the acquaintance? However this may be, a shot from my gun cuts their reflections short, and they make off at a bound, leaving behind them one of the number which I have wounded, and which cannot keep up with the main body.

On returning to camp I learn that Niaz is ill, and that nearly all the men are complaining of headache. Above our heads are a number of crows which have followed in the track of the pilgrims and fed upon their dead, while we also notice some rats

23

of the species peculiar to the steppe. Larks, and other birds, including the *sha-ti* (sand-grouse), fly through the air at a great pace, as if anxious to get out of such an inhospitable region.

December 15.—We cross the chain of hills and make our way towards the peaks, doing our best to find easy going, and to avoid the marshes and ravines. As soon as possible we steered a southerly course, and only discovered that we were on a sort of terrace, an immense tableland above the plains, when we got to the edge of it. In descending the slope we were surprised to see a regular flock of *orongos* which were browsing in the bed of a torrent, silvered in places by layers of salt that seemed like pools of water or blocks of ice. Having no skins of these antelopes, which we had never seen before, we lost no time in killing some. It would be impossible to conceive anything more graceful than the way in which these animals carry themselves, combining so much elegance with so much strength. We admire their large black muzzles, their broad dark chests, their grey coats, and the fury with which the males attack one another.

The females get their young together and drive them up towards the hills, galloping after them at a great pace. The males, now on the flanks of the herd, now in the rear, and now going back to fetch one of the females which has lagged behind, bound along, head downwards, with an agility which we envy all the more because we cannot go more than twenty yards without sitting down to rest. These antelopes display a certain amount of courage, for a male which Prince Henry had shot charged him, and had to be despatched with a revolver, while one which I had wounded tried to rip open the horse which Rachmed, who went close up to it, was riding. Father Dedeken also killed one, and the result of all this is that, being delayed in our march, we cannot reach the frozen pool, and have to go to bed without drinking. We give this plain the name of the antelopes (*Orongos*) we have killed here, and it is to be hoped that any future explorer who may fail to see any *orongos* in these parts will not tax us with exaggeration.

December 16.—The whole of our troop was astir early, and lost no time in reaching the frozen river which supplies the snowy chain trending eastward. We shelter ourselves from the north-west wind at the foot of a terrace, and the day is spent in eating and drinking. A few delicacies are distributed by way of dessert, and with the sun warming us a little in the afternoon, good-humour is restored. All the sick persons, except Niaz, are improving. Parpa, who was constantly groaning, looks much brighter, and Rachmed assures me that there was not really much the matter with him. I hear my companions making all sorts of plans, and I am myself inclined to regard them as feasible. In the meanwhile it is decided not to start in future without two or three days' supply of ice and a corresponding quantity of *argol*. The reader can have no idea how difficult it is to induce men who are tired out to take the most primitive precautions against cold and thirst. We are encamped at an altitude of 15,400 feet, and, looking back towards the north, we can again see the Columbus mountains. It seems as if we were separated from them by a smooth plain cut in two by a long ridge of cliffs.

December 17.—Winding round the chain of hills which protected us, and leaving on our left, to the east, the snow-capped mountains, we arrived by a small pass at the camping-ground of the Kalmucks, on the brink of a dried-up torrent, the carcases of five camels indicating the route to follow. The stage was a fatiguing one, owing to a blinding nor'-wester. We followed an easy path, winding along the spurs of hills, many of which terminate at their culminating point in protuberances like warts on the human body.

Before making for the south-west we saw behind us, from the top of the pass, the hill of which we had first of all made the circuit. Its summit is jagged and broken up into battlements of

Asiatic aspect, while it bristles with sharp points in the shape of arrows and Gothic steeples.

December 18.—All night the abominable north-west wind has been howling, with a minimum of 9° below zero. The men are all ill, with the usual symptoms. When we prepared for a start the thermometer was at 2° below zero, with a good deal of wind, and it was no pleasant business for the men to handle the ropes. We were still in a desert of sand and stones, with a few tufts of rank grass and salt, but after scrambling over a pass about 16,000 feet above the sea-level, with our camels, we descended into the valley through a gorge, where we get welcome protection from the wind. We believe that we are now on the other side of the Prjevalsky chain, and, according to Timour, this chain extends as far as Bokalik.

We halt in the midst of the sand, in a hollow where we can set the wind at defiance. All around us the ground undulates very much, and the horizon is so far familiar that we can make out the same peaks which have hitherto served as landmarks, though we believe we are in another region. Presently the wind goes down and the sky becomes overcast. At nightfall, and with the temperature at only 3° above zero, we find it so pleasant that we call this place the Camp de la Miséricorde.

December 19.—To give further justification for this name, we were informed on waking this morning that nearly all our men were indisposed, especially Imatch the bandy-legged. They attributed this indisposition to a hot wind which, they said, was blowing during the night. As to Niaz, he is so weak that he cannot stand up, and the men say this hot wind must have been very bad for him. Yet the thermometer stood as low as 18° below zero during the night. Soon there is a fall of snow, but only for a few minutes; then the sun comes out, and it would be just the weather for starting on the march, only we have no horses. They had been picketed out before daybreak, so as to enable them to graze upon the scanty herbage, but the poor animals, not having drunk for several days, went off in quest of a spring. As the reader may imagine, they had some distance to travel, and Timour, who went off in search of them, has not returned. Night sets in, and still there are no signs of him. Rachmed has been scouring the country, and has found traces of Kalmucks going directly south through the sands. As soon as it gets dark a lantern is hoisted at the top of a pole and placed on a hillock, so that it may serve as a lighthouse for Timour. At intervals we fire off a gun or a revolver. All our men are haunted with the idea that he is calling out, and at intervals one of them gets up and fires off his gun. So it goes on all night.

December 20.—At 5 a.m. there is a fall of about half an inch of snow, as fine as sleet, and the temperature rises a little. The sky remains overcast, and then a south-west wind gets up and the sun comes out. The minimum for the night has been 25° below zero, and we feel very sorry for poor Timour, who has not yet returned. Parpa starts off on a camel, carrying a pelisse, some food, and water in the shape of ice, and he goes to the left, while Rachmed sets out to the right on foot, carrying a cudgel, a revolver, and some bread. He will go as far as he can, for not only is Timour his friend, but he realises what a disaster the loss of the horses would be. We watch him start at the rapid pace which his familiarity with life on lofty mountains alone renders possible, and await the result with no little anxiety.

About noon Timour arrived, on Parpa's camel, the latter following at a slower rate with the horses. We welcomed him back with delight, and he had tears in his eyes when he saw us again, being blue with cold and very tired. After he had consumed a good deal of tea and sugar, he related his adventures as follows :—

"I found the track of the horses two hours after leaving the camp. First of all, they had gone somewhat at haphazard, wandering from right to left, and then one of them assumed the lead taking the others a great distance. It was not till close upon the feeding-time for animals in winter (about three o'clock) that I caught sight of the first horse. I got on his back in order to reach the others, but finding that he was tired, I got off and led him. I gradually caught them all, beginning with those which were the most tired, and as I caught them I hobbled them with their halters. Then when I had secured them all—for I counted them—I got them together, and night set in. I marched on, driving them in front of me, but, despite the brilliancy of the stars, I could not find the camp. I called out, but could get no answer, so I tied the horses together and slept leaning against one of them which had lain down. This warmed me a little, but it was bitterly cold, and I have a pain in my head."

Everyone was overjoyed, for Timour is very much liked, no work being too much for him, while he is one of the best men we have to follow out a track. When travelling, one soon gets attached to men of this type, and soon learns in the same way to despise the selfish and the lazy.

The first thing was to give the horses water. First of all, we tried to obtain some by cutting into the ice of a small lake near our camp, but it was only a waste of time; for though we hacked and hewed away, there was no sign of any water. Then we piled up roots and *argol*, to which we set fire, passing the whole day in melting the ice, so as to distribute small quantities of water to the poor animals. This operation lasted all the afternoon and part of the evening; in future, whenever we get into camp, we will cut blocks of ice out of the surface of the lakes and let the horses crunch them.

In the afternoon we saw larks and other birds flying eastwards and rats emerging from the ground, attracted by the sunlight. In going to look for Rachmed—as it is he who is lost now—I climbed to the summit of a sandhill, the smooth base of which is scored by rugged lines forming one of a series of hillocks which remind me of *barkhans*,* which have been brought to a stand-still. In the first place, plants with an infinite growth of roots have enveloped them as it were in a web, then tufts of grass have fixed them in their place. The snow as it melted has acted like masonry, and the wind has ceased to have any hold except upon the very light grains which are sprinkled on the surface.

The snow has streaked with white this corner of the earth's surface, and the sun has, if I may so express myself, made the landscape look old-fashioned, like that which you see on a box of sweetmeats. The colours are in juxtaposition, but they do not fuse, the effect being that of the chromo-lithographer rather than of the colourist. In all directions the soil has been scored by ephemeral torrents, which have left a little ice behind them in some corner or gully. At each step one takes it becomes clear that this is not a country in which it would be possible to live, for the solitude is too great, and the cold too intense. The lungs either do not act at all, or act too much, and if one happens to un-cover the mouth while walking, the bronchial tube is inflamed or irritated by the cold air. Most of our men are coughing during the night, and everything gets so dry that our toe- and finger-nails snap off at the least touch, while wood breaks like glass. The beard does not grow, but loses its colour, the hands chap, the skin cracks, and the lips swell. None of us escape the moun-tain sickness, to combat which great energy is required, for it saps all one's strength; and experience has shown me that the only way to obtain normal circulation of the blood is simply to keep moving quickly about after one has well lined one's stomach.

It is difficult to do anything on an empty stomach, for you at once have cold feet and a bad headache. As soon as you have

---

* Turkish name for hillocks of shifting sand.

taken food you feel better, and as you believe the mischief is past, and you are weak, you are tempted to lie down and wrap yourself well up. Your feet again get cold, and the headache returns, but as soon as you sit up you feel relieved, and if you go out for a quick walk the symptoms quickly disappear.

I have tried this several times upon myself and my men, and it has always been successful. It proved so to-day in the case of Imatch, who was complaining of a horrible headache till I made him take a good cup of tea with plenty of sugar, dipping into it a bit of bread as hard as a stone, and then go out and look for the sheep. He had a difficulty in making a start, but when he came back he was feeling better. It was the same with Iça and Parpa, and I have noticed that there were always more men ill on the days that we halted. First of all I thought this must be due to the reaction following on great fatigue, but I afterwards ascertained that it was because the men gave way and remained without motion, instead of facilitating the circulation of the blood by exercise.

While I am noting down this fact, the lighted lantern is once more hoisted to the top of our pole, Rachmed not having returned. Some of our men have been sent out to look for him, but they have returned without finding him, having been forbidden to go very far, for fear they might get lost themselves. Well as we are acquainted with Rachmed's ability, and confident as we feel that he has not lost his way, we begin to be anxious about him. He must have gone a great distance and been overtaken by the darkness. We fire guns at intervals, and utter prolonged shouts, for the cold is intense, with gusts of wind from the south-west, and the poor fellow only took a light cloak with him so as to be able to walk with comfort. At eight p.m. the thermometer marks 20° below zero, while the minimum of the night is 28° below zero, with a wind which freezes the blood in one's veins.

It may seem singular that our people should lose their way so often; but it will be neither the first nor the last time, nothing being easier even for the most prudent and experienced. It is difficult to imagine how hard it is to find one's way among these highlands, where a man loses all sense of perspective, his eye wandering over immense spaces without seeing, at given distances, either trees, houses, human beings, animals, or edifices the height of which is known to him. It is by the incessant and unconscious comparison of such objects as these that he has learned to form an idea of distance.

Here in the desert we have in a few weeks lost this sense of distance which we had gained by the experience of our lifetime. All that one sees is so alike: one hill is like another; according to the time of day a frozen pool either sparkles in the sun or disappears, so that one does not know whether it is large or small; a little bird fluttering its wings upon a clod of earth looks like a wild animal which has been lying down and is getting up; a crow flying away with its prey in the morning mist seems to be a gigantic condor carrying off a lamb in its claws, while at sunset this same crow, cleaning itself on the summit of a rock, looks the size of a yak or a bear.

And so the man who has lost sight of the caravan or camp is constantly being deceived. His eyes are affected by the smoke of the *argol*, the cold, the wind, and by having used them too much, and he is led astray by appearances. If the light fades, or the sky becomes overcast, he is lost. Night overtakes him—a black and starless night—and then he has only one thing to do, viz., to stay where he is until either the wind clears away the clouds, or the moon gets up, or until day dawns again. Should the sky clear before dawn, he may endeavour to make for his camp by means of the polar star. Or in the morning the sun will tell him where the east is. But a man must be very bold, or have a marvellous memory for the direction followed, to trust himself merely to the cardinal points. The surest, not to say the only

24

way, is to retrace one's steps, and should they have been effaced by a tempest, the man may be regarded as lost.

All night long I hear the groans of Niaz, who is very ill and cannot recover. He is delirious, fancying that he can see two children holding his head. He complains of intolerable pains in the brain, and has no strength to eat or drink, while his tongue is swollen, his face and lips being tumefied and blue. We can do nothing for him; what he wants is to be at a lower altitude, and we shall probably be obliged to mount still higher to-morrow.

December 21.—This morning, Rachmed not having returned, Dedeken on horseback and Timour on a camel went to meet him, and soon returned followed by Rachmed, who, after mounting the camel, felt the cold a good deal, and preferred to walk. He does not seem to be very much done up; and after he has eaten and drunk heartily, we hear his story. He has been a long way, describing a large semicircle around the traces of a route, and as he saw nothing he went marching on until he got surprised by night. Then, thanks to a clear sky, he came upon the track of the Mongols, and rested for a little beside a fire of *argol* which he lighted. "Then," he went on to say, "I returned in the direction of the camp, and the cold was so intense that I no longer dared to stop for fear of going to sleep and never waking again. So then I warmed myself again in my own way."

" How did you manage ? "

" I unrolled the strips of wool which I had round my feet and legs, and put half of them next to my chest, under my clothes; and when I stopped to rest, I removed the strips I had round my feet, and substituted for them those which had been warmed by contact with my body. So I could stop for a minute without having my feet frozen. When the cold began to get trying, I started off again, and walked nearly the whole night."

We were delighted to see him back, and after a few minutes' rest, he was at work again as usual. He even wanted to strike our tents and establish the camp further on, where there is a little grass, but it being late, we deferred the operation till to-morrow.

It is a consolation to know that there is no one missing, for we are so isolated in this immense desert that the very worst of our men is extremely precious. Perhaps this may be because man is scarce, and his value, like that of other things, is a question of supply and demand. But it is not merely for economic reasons that we are full of anxiety when one of our men is missing. It is because we are attached to him, because he belongs to our troop, to our party. When travelling, I have often watched the flocks of birds flying overhead, and going in families and troops like ourselves. I imagine that when they meet in the evening and compose themselves to sleep, each head of the family counts his flock, and if one is missing the companions of the absent one are all in distress. So is it with us.

December 22.—During the night there were gusts of wind from the south-west, with a minimum of 22° below zero. A horse has died, the first of the long series which must inevitably follow. After having passed several sandy mountain spurs, we reached a large valley, extending from north-west to south-east. The sand, dotted with tufts of grass, was succeeded by denuded and stony surfaces, which appeared to have been washed bare by torrential floods.

All at once there arose to our right, westward, at a point where the chain we have before us seems to join on to that which we have left behind, what looked like the peak of Stromboli, as I saw it for the first time when making for Sicily. Looking downward, I saw that the bed of the ravines we were going through was darkish in hue and sprinkled about with lava. We encamped in the lava plain, and christened the volcano, which let fall its long trailing mantle just west of us, after Reclus, the greatest of French geographers, who will be pleased to hear of our discovery. East-ward, amid a number of snowy peaks, there towers a giant more than 23,000 feet high, which we named after Ferrier, a French traveller little known to his countrymen, who, in his day, made a magnificent journey through Afghanistan. This valley is, of course, shut in by mountains, and it strikes us as being about a hundred miles long. To the north, the chain undulates in some places, and is jagged in others; westward, we notice several cones beyond the Reclus volcano.

We have to go to bed without lighting a fire, and therefore without drinking any tea, as the roots we have picked up are too impregnated with salt to produce a flame. Niaz is dying.

A good many *orongo* antelopes are in sight, and wolves and foxes are prowling about. They seem. to live principally upon a small grey rodent with a large head, not unlike a guinea-pig.

December ·23.—A cold wind from the south-east, with a minimum of 22° below zero. When we started southward, where there appeared to be a pass leading through the chain, the sky was clear. The desert, up which we made our way by a very gradual ascent, was bare and stony, furrowed by a few ravines, within which *orongos* were lying sheltered, beside large slabs of salt. At our feet were cinders, lava, and a very dark surface, and the pass, wide where we entered it, gradually narrowed. But the route was a good one for the camels, being soft to the feet and dusty, with bits of schist lying about. As soon as we lost sight of the Reclus volcano there was an end to the lava.

The Dungan is in a bad humour. This morning he beat his son and wanted to kill him, Rachmed being compelled to intervene. As to Niaz, he has become unconscious, and is strapped on to a camel to prevent him from falling off. When I came into the camp after all the others, I learned that when the Dungan got there he did not even make the camel kneel down, but, unfastening the ropes, let Niaz fall with all his weight to the ground. This heartlessness, which is characteristic of the Chinese race, is a thing to which neither we nor our

BURIAL OF NIAZ.

Mussulmans can accustom ourselves. It is just as well not to have a revolver about one when present at such scenes as this.

Our camp is pitched in the middle of the pass, at an altitude of about 17,340 feet, and it is bitterly cold. The wind has swept a little snow into the crevices, and this is carefully collected, some of it being given to the men, while the rest is put into the canoes, which will serve as drinking-troughs for our horses. They swallow the snow, which we have mixed with barley, with manifest satisfaction.

Niaz is at the last gasp, his face being hardly recognisable, and he cannot open his eyes. About six o'clock Timour comes to say that he thinks he is dead, but Rachmed finds that he is still breathing, though he cannot get through the night.

December 24.—At daybreak the tempest which had begun in the night is still raging; and Rachmed, when he comes to make his customary report, has a depressed look, with tears standing in his eyes. "It is all over," he says, "with Niaz, but we have neither water nor wood to melt the ice, and we cannot wash the body according to the rite, nor array it in clean garments."

"No matter; Allah will forgive you, for you are doing the best you can."

"We will roll the body up in the white felt which I lent him to keep himself warm. But I do not think we can dig him a grave. The mountain is too hard."

"Inter him the best way you can."

"I will do so myself, with the help of Timour, who is reciting the prayers, and of Parpa, who has sat at meat with Niaz's sister."

"Very good; we will help you too."

The body of the faithful servant, which has been stiffened by the cold, lies wrapped up in the pelisse near the tent of his ill-conditioned master, and we cover it with white felt. The snow is falling in whirling flakes all around us, and the wind is piercingly cold, as our men take their pickaxes and try to break up the ground. This they fail to do, and then they see what can be done with their hatchets, for the Mussulmans are not like the Buddhists, who leave their dead exposed, and they would give anything to put the body of Niaz beyond reach of the wild beasts. But the effort they make soon takes their breath away, and they have to stop and rest, the tears which run down their cheeks freezing on their beards, from which they hang like so many icicles. They are soon exhausted, for the tempest takes all their breath away, and they have only been able to make a very shallow grave—little more than one of those cavities which animals scoop out with their paws when they want to go to sleep.

Then Rachmed remembers that the dead man's face should be turned towards the holy city of Mecca, and he is afraid whether all this labour may not have been in vain. So he questions Parpa on the point; but Timour has thought of the Keblah, and, pointing to the south-west he says, " It is over there, we can place him so."

Rachmed asks me if the needle of the compass tells the same story, and, upon my saying that it does, they take up the body carefully, lay it on the ground as a mother might her sleeping child, and raise the head, which is well covered up, on to a flat stone, so that, as they think, Niaz may sleep better. They tuck him in as if he were in bed, and are surprised to find as they move him how illness has brought down his weight. Then, when he is carefully put to rest, they place the stones and the lumps of earth over him, and go on until the whole of the felt, which serves as a coffin for him, is hidden from sight. Then each of us, in order to complete the work, gets a slab of schist out of the pocket of his cloak and places it over the grave, while Timour plants in the ground several straight pieces of wood at the place where the head is laid. That done, we have to say farewell to our worthy comrade. Father Dedeken first recites some prayers, and is followed by Timour. We are all of us sobbing, and Timour can scarcely finish his oration, which he winds up in a paroxysm of grief by affirming the greatness of Allah, the survivors taking up the refrain, " Allah is great ! God is great ! "

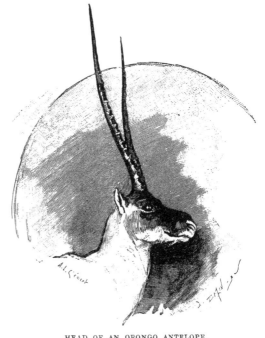

So we commit to his rest, each of us after our own customs and with sincere sorrow, sterling, honest Niaz.

Then the camels are loaded amid the violent snowstorm, and when all is ready the Dungan, who had treated his servant worse than a camel, comes and prostrates himself ceremoni-

HEAD OF AN ORONGO ANTELOPE.

ously, as befits a representative of the best bred people in Asia—I mean, of course, the Chinese.

When we start, the *bouran* becomes more intense, and it being hopeless to think of following out a track in such weather, we have to guess our way until the sun, after being so long veiled behind the clouds, comes out and gives us fresh courage. We reach the summit of the pass, and deviate a little eastwards to a gully, down which we go protected from all wind, and in which we can feel the warmth of the sun, our gloomy feelings evaporating under its cheering influence.

After coming out of the gully and crossing the chain where

25

the body of Niaz is interred, we again find ourselves in a valley analogous to the " Valley of Lava," but not so long or so broad, and extending eastward, with lakes—some of which are close to salt deposits—that appear to be frozen over. There is a succession of dried beds of torrents, bare hills, and wandering *orongos,* with snow accumulated in some of the crevices. This is the only modification to which the scenery, that varies so little in this region, is subject. The sky being cloudy, our horizon is an extremely limited one, and the traces of the pilgrims grow scarcer and scarcer, being only visible where the camels have left their droppings.

December 25.—To-day there is a fall of snow. We see nothing but small lakes, salt, and sandy hills. One pass is very much like another, and when the sky is clear we can see mountain upon mountain, with a great variety of peaks, and a mixture of ice and snow. The route is strewn with the dead bodies of yaks, which had belonged to the Kalmucks, and the snow falls nearly every day, though in small quantities, the wind blowing from the south-west; and we have quite lost our way.

December 29.—The wind is to the west, and this does not mend our case, for we are going due south over a bare plain. We encamp in the midst of the lava, at the foot of a volcano to which we give the name of Ruysbruk, or Rubruquis, in compliment to the great Flemish traveller, the compatriot of Father Dedeken. To the west of the camp, Prince Henry and Timour come upon camel-droppings, so the route which goes southward is again found. The marches are now very severe, for, in addition to the twelve miles or so of mountain climbing we do each day, the route for the following one has to be prospected. As soon as the tent has been pitched, sometimes while it is being pitched, we go forward to see what lies before us, a slice of bread and a few dried apricots helping to keep one in trim. But it is tiring work, for no sooner do we get to what looks like a summit than we find there is a higher one beyond, and in this way we are often tempted on and on until night sets in, with difficulty finding our way back to the camp.

After a still, starry night, with a minimum of 21° below zero, we started just as a west wind, still more intolerable than yesterday's, got up. We could not open our right eyes, and it was the same with the horses, whose right eyes were masked by a frozen tear. Vestiges of the preceding year were very apparent in the plain. The "Red Pass," as we call it, because of the colour of the soil, led us to the camp of the pilgrims, which had been pitched in a depression of the ground behind a volcano, of which there is a whole series just here. The wind did not stop till about seven p.m., and we notice that this west wind generally rises about ten a.m.

December 30.—The night having been a quiet one, the men say they feel better, and the weather is now magnificent. To the north-west a volcano stands out very clear and distinct, capped with snow, and the sun sheds upon the scene a tinge of the picturesque to which our eye is not accustomed. For four hours we pass a good deal of lava, the largest blocks being the farthest from the volcano, close to which there is a good deal of crumbling dust.

At first our route is a pleasant one, following a well-sheltered narrow ravine, in which it is quite warm. But this is too good to last, and we come out upon the steppe across which a bitter wind is blowing. Before the hurricane has reached its maximum of intensity I have time to distinguish in the west a vast chain of mountains with snowy peaks thirty or thirty-five miles away, so far as I can judge with my eyes so inflamed.

At times, we cannot see ten paces in front of us, and I have the camels brought close together, Prince Henry putting himself at their head and leading them, by means of the compass, in a southerly direction. Rachmed and myself endeavour to find the traces of the route, and the others shelter themselves as best they can behind the camels.

The tempest is gradually demolishing the crumbling hills and the *barkhans* in the lower grounds. The laws of gravity prevail even here, and while at the foot of the hills we are assailed by what might be described as grains of corn: higher up, there is a dust which forms into waves and which the tempest lifts and hurls in all directions. The scene is a fantastic one, and these mountains of sand form a singular spectacle. In the evening, we come upon the pilgrims' camping-ground in a " haven," within which we are glad to take rest.

December 31.—The tempest lasted all through the night, with a minimum of 21° below zero. We sorely need a lower altitude, for men, horses, and camels are alike in a bad way, and old Imatch has one of his feet badly swollen. All through this the last day of the year we marched along between sandhills, winding round the shores of a lake, our horses pretty well blinded by the dust and sand. The camels would not follow one another, for the wind blinded and stupefied them, and each one tried to shelter himself behind the other. This caused them to deviate from the straight line, and Prince Henry, with compass in hand, leading the way, had constantly to turn round and put the caravan straight.

It is thus that we reached the camping-ground and found an *ad libitum* supply of *argol* and ice. This makes the encampment just tolerable, and we celebrate the New Year by slaughtering a sheep which has lost most of its fat, but which is none the less appreciated. Imatch, whose foot has swollen in an alarming way, complains of headache and singing in the ears. Being afraid that the foot is frost-bitten, we apply a plaster made of mutton fat; he also puts his foot into the smoking paunch of the sheep, which at once gives him relief.

Iça prepares a dish which is not at all inviting in appearance,

but tastes better than it looks : it is made out of the sheep's
entrails.   Then we make an immense *tchouzma*, this consisting
of flour mixed with mutton fat, which is boiled in a small quantity
of water, a little powdered sugar being then added.   After great
difficulty we get a little tea, for the wind is so violent that it
takes hours to melt the ice and boil the water, just as the meat
cannot be thoroughly cooked for the same reason.   Then, after
expressing our best wishes for a happy new year to our relatives
and friends at home, and securing the pegs of our tent, which
the wind assails with unabated fury, we turn in as quickly as
possible, Prince Henry trying to put the best face on things by
observing that in such weather as this one would not be better
off at sea.

CHAPTER VIII.

A WILDERNESS OF MOUNTAINS.

New Year's Greetings--The Ruysbruk Volcano—Abdullah Astray—Recovering the Track of the Pilgrims—Making for the Tengri Nor—Crossing the Lake of Cones on the Ice—"Lake Montcalm"—A Valley of Dry Bones—The Dupleix Mountains—Human Handiwork—Probable Source of the Yang-tse-Kiang—Fossils at a Height of 19,000 Feet—Traces of Human Beings—40° Below Zero—Celebrating the Chinese New Year—"Crows with a Metallic Croak"—Mountains Everywhere—Running Water.

THE PRINCE IN HIS TRAVELLING OUTFIT.

January 1, 1890.—After having exchanged greetings, we are delighted to find that the hurricane from the west has subsided to a wind which we should have thought intolerable four or five days ago, but which we now regard as little more than an ordinary breeze. The sky is comparatively clear, and the year opens auspiciously. We can make out where we are, and to the N.N.W the Ruysbruk volcano stands out so distinctly that one might imagine it had got closer to us. Snowy peaks, visible in all directions, show that we have got out of the desert. As we could not detect any traces of the pilgrims, we steered due south.

We emerged from the sandy valley to encamp on the hills, not far from the ice, and sheltered from the west wind. The soil is covered with lava, and is of a very dark hue, the presence of all this lava being accounted for by the proximity of several cones of volcanoes. As soon as we arrived we broke up into small parties to search for the traces of the pilgrims' route, but found none. At nightfall Abdullah was missing.

January 2.—Abdullah did not return all night, to our great disquietude, and this morning Rachmed and Timour went in search of him. Rachmed brought back his horse, without its saddle or piece of felt, and soon after Abdullah himself followed in a pitiable state. He had got astray in the storm, his horse had dropped out of sheer weakness, and, after having made a vain attempt to return, he had unsaddled the beast and taken its piece of felt to cover himself with. Having plenty of *argol* handy, he had lighted a fire with the butt end of his whip, and would have passed the night in comparative comfort had he not been so terribly hungry. But he soon made up for lost time.

After the comparative lull during the night and morning, the west wind got up again about nine o'clock, but fortunately the soil where we are is not very sandy. So we do not suffer so much from the dust, though in the valley below it blows in such clouds that there is nothing else to be seen.

When I go down to the banks of the stream to see if I cannot discover some traces of a route, I come upon the tracks of a wolf, and soon after the wolf himself appears, in pursuit of a herd of antelopes. He has not much chance of overtaking them, and when he stops short, a bullet from my rifle rudely breaks in upon his reflections.

There is a good deal of animal life about, larks, black eagles, and falcons hovering in the air, and I notice that there are a great many animals of the rat species, which have their holes in the slopes. They are light grey in colour, with large heads, powerful jaws, long bodies, and short legs. They seem to be fat and comfortable, and I am almost tempted to envy them their warm holes in this bitter weather.

At nightfall Rachmed came in from the south without having discovered the least trace of the passage of the pilgrims.

Father Dedeken has been equally unsuccessful, and so, too, has Prince Henry, who came in dead tired, carrying on his back the heads of two *orongos* which he had killed. Timour was still absent, and it was not for a long time, and after we had been shouting for him in all directions, that he made his appearance, with icicles hanging from his beard, and so done up that he could hardly stand. He had difficulty in breathing and in getting out his words, but his face was radiant, for he had come upon plenty of traces, in proof of which he proudly produced some camel-droppings from his pocket.

This piece of news puts all our troop in good humour, especially as the droppings are so similar to those we have seen before that they clearly belong to the same camels.

January 3.—We make rather to the east, so as to strike the pilgrims' route. Enormous yaks stand to watch us pass, and but for the disobedience of a dog, we might have killed one of these mountains of flesh. A camel which had seemed to be quite well died suddenly as we were climbing one of the many hills up and down which we went all day in this region so full of ravines. In the evening we find shelter in the bottom of a small amphitheatre of hills, amid the crumbling sandstone. The cliffs and banks, eaten out and scored by the wind, break the usual monotony of our horizon, and produce the effect of a country which is inhabited, or which has been.

The sky is clear, the west wind has dropped almost completely, and, with the moon shining brightly, we shall have a sharp night.

January 5.—The thermometer marked a minimum of 35° below zero, and the morning is a lovely one. I need not describe our route, for it is always the same, up hill and down dale, its monotony being broken only by the west wind, which seems always to get up about ten a.m.

It is as bitterly cold as ever, and after marching for

some time, we see to the south, above a dark but not very lofty chain of hills, a number of icy peaks all in a line. They form part of a very high and jagged chain, covered with snow,

THE RUYSBRUK PEAK.

and some of our men want to know how we are to cross this mass of snow and ice, declaring that the farther we advance the more intense is the cold and the higher are the mountains. One chain after another bars the way, and how are we to get over them? I endeavour to console them by pointing to the horizon behind us, and to the mountains, which look just as impassable as those in front of us.

We shall have some good tea this evening, for we have come upon a lake—in shape resembling a double eye-glass—with ice as pure as crystal, so we empty our sacks of the dirty ice they contained and take in a fresh supply. Pitching our camp in the lowest part of the valley near the lake, our arrival puts to flight a dozen *orongos* licking the surface of the ice, which shone in the sun like a mirror, and reflected their graceful forms. There are blocks of lava along the edge of this lake, the level of which

26

has been gradually falling, for we can trace six successive circles on the banks, indicating the six successive changes of level. It seems certain, too, that there are some hot water springs nearly in the centre.

The night is magnificent, and as I walk along the shores of this little lake, it sparkles almost as much as the moon, having, besides, a white halo of salt upon its banks. Our tent is pitched in a regular basin, while above us the lava has the appearance of a herd of cattle lying down, or of dark-plumaged birds waiting to swoop down upon some corpse. The stillness is unbroken until a camel, which is very thirsty, gets up and goes to drink, finding, much to his disappointment, that it is ice and not water on the surface. In due course he goes back and lies down beside his companions, and again the stillness is complete, except for the sort of humming sound in the ears peculiar to high altitudes.

Owing to the dryness of the air, the light falls in floods upon the hollow where we have our camp, projecting my shadow clearly upon the salt. When I get back to the tent, the thermometer marks 29° below zero. Prince Henry reminds Father Dedeken that they had come upon the traces of a wolf before turning in, and they suggest that as I am up, I should go in search of it.

January 6.—The thermometer marks 40° below zero, the point at which the mercury freezes, and there is still the west wind. We are surrounded to the north-west with lava apparently vomited from the mouth of a crater.

Loading our animals and starting southward, we came upon a pool of water about twenty minutes afterwards, at the sight of which, horses, camels, sheep, and dogs, got into a state of great excitement, only to find that the water was so salt and brackish that they could not drink it. The enormous quantity of salt had kept the water liquid, but the poor animals could not know this, of course, and some of our men thought it might be hot springs which had prevented it from freezing.

I had omitted to say that we have given up looking for traces of the pilgrims, as the search gave more trouble than it was worth, and it may be that this route extends too much to the east, for we do not wish to come out by the grand route of the Koukou Nor, followed by Fathers Huc and Gabet, and afterwards by Prjevalsky. We are endeavouring to make the lake of Tengri Nor, trying to keep rather to its right than its left as we go southward. Marching on in front of the caravan as pioneers, my companions and myself do not intend to go after game except in so far as we require it for food and for our collections, our main object being to trace a route of our own without any sort of guide.

In the evening we encamp about a quarter of a mile from a fine piece of water which we call " the Lake of Cones," because of the shape of the mountains which surround it. We try to pierce the ice of a small pool to let the animals drink, but they cut themselves about the mouth. The horses remained for three hours munching the pieces of ice.

January 7.—We crossed the ice of the Lake of Cones in forty minutes. The south-west end of it does not seem to be frozen; it is about twelve miles long by two broad. After going over a rather steep pass, we descended into a deserted valley, where we killed a few hares, which, if small, are of excellent flavour. During the last few days we have seen nothing of any big game, and yet there has been very little snow and a certain quantity of grass, such as it is. Their absence may be due to the persistent winds or the great height, the blast of the tempest and an altitude of 18,000 feet not constituting any great attraction.

The day has been cheerful, even for the most gloomy of our men, for the Dungan himself, inasmuch as we have come upon wood that had been fashioned by human hands, and upon saddle-bows for yaks, made of juniper wood. This discovery led to all sorts of comments, and while they were being made, the Dungan came up smiling, although he has had to abandon another of his camels to-day, and said that he has seen some *argols* which had been turned over, this being done so that they might dry, a proof that the men who have done this intend to return. He invited Abdullah and several of the other men to come and eat some of his dough, and congratulated himself upon the prospect of celebrating the Chinese New Year, which is in thirteen days' time, under the shelter of a roof.

These hopes improve the *morale* of our men for a few days, but we know the old saying about "hope deferred," and it takes little to provoke a revulsion of feeling when men are worn out and cut off from the world of their fellows.

January 8.—The scouts we sent out came back and told us that, beyond the second chain of mountains, there is a large lake. This we go and inspect to-day, to find that it is not frozen over, and that its western extremity is about twenty-five miles off. Judging by the gaps we see in the midst of the mountains, we shall encounter a good many lakes, and it is only to be hoped that they are frozen over, and that we shall not be obliged to go out of our way to get round them.

We are at the mercy of the waves, so to speak, being on a boundless ocean, the billows of which keep rising before us in the shape of mountains, and our troop is made up of a number of swimmers tired of breasting wave after wave only to find a higher one before them.

After following a narrow valley, in which are a number of salt water springs, we reached the extremity of the lake, which is gradually drying up, as we crossed what was formerly part of it, but is now covered with a foot of salt. We imagined that we had got to the end of the lake, but upon breasting an eminence we recognised our mistake, as the hills had hidden from our view another stretch of water. We gave the name of Mont-calm to this fine piece of water, which extends from east to west for a length of forty-five or fifty miles. The islands and peninsulas prevent us from calculating its precise breadth, but we put it at from six to twelve miles. This water delights the eye, and gives one the illusion of the sea-shore, its aspect being particularly beautiful when, at sunset, the westerly wind causes its sparkling surface to undulate like the silvery scales of a fish.

January 9.—Winding our way round Lake Montcalm towards the south-east, we saw a great many wild animals, such as yaks, *koulans*, *arkars*, and even the chamois of the Himalayas; and we cheered up our men by pointing to the presence of animals which are indigenous to the frontiers of India.

Beyond a small pass, we came upon some hot-water springs, but they were salt, and upon a frozen river which, as seen through the mist, appears to be flowing south-east through a vast plain.

Can this stream be flowing towards China? At once our thoughts revert to the sources of the great Blue River. We cannot say if we have lighted upon them, but in any case we can assert that it is somewhere in this direction that they must be sought. The idea that this ice feeds rivers which shed their waters in the Pacific Ocean seems to bring us back into contact with the world, for if our supposition is correct, all we should have to do would be to follow down the course of this stream to the coast.

January 10.—We had to see after the feet of our camels and to shoe our horses. The minimum yesterday was 26 below zero, while last night it was only 13 below, and this morning 2 above, zero, temperatures which to us seem delicious.

In the afternoon, Prince Henry came back to camp for a camel to bring in the body of a yak which he had killed by lodging eight bullets in him. We took out the necessary instru-ments for skinning and cutting him up, and when we came upon him about three-quarters of a mile from the camp, found that he must be one of the seniors of Thibet, his muzzle being quite grey, his teeth worn, and his skin half-tanned by age. It was no easy matter to skin him, and he was so heavy that it was as much as a camel could do to carry him.

The sky was clouded over all day, and had very much the same appearance as in the region of the Lob Nor, this moisture of the air being due to the proximity of Lake Montcalm, off which the wind blows.

Two of the horses died during the evening from having drunk too much water. It is fortunate they were the only two which discovered these springs, or we should have lost them all. The camels are none the worse for having drunk; but, they have only been allowed a limited quantity, and our drivers think that the bladder has contracted with all our animals, and that the slightest excess of drinking will be fatal. Imatch holds that it will be better not to water the camels at the hot springs if we come upon any later.

January 12.—We are in a valley strewn with the bones of animals, such as *arkars*, *koulans*, yaks, *orongos*, and *Nemorhedus Edwardi.** We can only guess the cause of so many skeletons being assembled in one place. It may have been an epidemic, or a very severe winter, or it may be that the aged animals of the flock chose to come here to die.

January 14.—We encamp at the foot of the pass which we shall have to scale in order to cross an enormous chain of mountains, which we name after that distinguished Frenchman, Dupleix.

The enthusiasm excited by the discovery of the piece of wood wrought by human hands has quite subsided, for we are at a

---

* A very interesting collection of animals, plants, etc., brought back by M. Bonvalot and his companions has been exhibited during the summer and autumn in the Natural History Museum, Paris.—*The Translator.*

greater altitude than ever, some of the peaks beside our camp being at least twenty thousand feet high, while for the last three days we have been groping for the path which will lead us to the other side of the chain, the solitude being deeper and weighing heavier than ever. There are numberless traces of wild animals and big game having been this way; but they have all cleared off, as if at the word of command, and we see nothing but a woebegone crow, which seems to follow us with interest.

Our men are out of heart, for there seems to be no end to these lofty tablelands, and the west wind blows incessantly. Rachmed tries to cheer them up, and talks of India as if it were just round the corner; but the conclusion of his discourse is very practical, for he says, "We have plenty of provisions; let us do like our horses, only look where we put down our feet, and go marching on."

January 15.—We cross a pass at about 16,500 feet, following a gentle slope, and to the west see the glaciers extending down to a valley, which we shall follow, marching over ice. In the mist we catch a glimpse of snowy peaks, which we calculate to be at least 26,000 feet high; and throughout the whole of this region there is a multiplicity of small lakes and pools. The hills, the soil of which is very friable, bear traces of the melting of the snows and of the inundations which follow, and there is abundance of ice.

January 18.—As we began our march, two days ago, over the frozen river, deep and broad, and its surface so slippery that our men could hardly keep their feet, we could not help thinking that the Dupleix mountains must be the origin of a great river, or, at all events, one of its principal sources.

When the snow has fallen in the course of the next few months and the sun has come to melt it, there will be a tremendous inundation of the highlands, which will be traversed by rivers of liquid mud, a good deal of which will be left upon the flanks of the hills; these deposits will remain there until the summer following, for winter arrests the flow of the river, when the sun acts, lique-fying the solid masses, which gradually break away and come down lower each year.

It is, of course, impossible to say positively, but my belief is

"PIC DE BUSSY."

that we are at the sources of the Yang-tse-Kiang. For some days past our men have been craving for the sight of their fellow-men, and all this because they caught sight of that bit of wood; they are constantly scanning the horizon, examining the soil, fancying they have discovered traces, and triumphantly announcing their " find " to the others, getting quite angry if you seek to prove that they are mistaken. I try to persuade them that they are wrong in desiring the presence of their fellow-men, that they have nothing good to expect from them, that it would be much better for us to be able quietly to continue our route, and that a few fat sheep, a little good drinking water, and an end of the west wind would be worth any number of Thibetans. But my reasons do not impress them, and nothing will satisfy them but to see men. After three days' slipping and tumbling on the surface of the river, which descends by a narrow defile, we have come out upon a plain, in the best of spirits, for we have made two or three discoveries which put everybody in good heart. Yesterday we found fossils at a height about 19,000 feet, while about two o'clock I came, in a well-sheltered gorge, upon a calcined stone, standing by itself, with horse-droppings all around. Lower down were other stones which had been placed side by side, for the lighting of a fire, which showed that man had been there. A fire of *argol* and roots had actually been lighted, and as the snow had not covered the ashes, this must have been done recently. Then I saw, clinging to the rock, a fragment of the skin of the megalo-partridge, with the feathers adhering to it, so shooters must have stopped there to take a meal. But they could not have passed the night here, for there was no trace of any shelter having been erected.

Our caravan came up soon after, and my powers of description would fail to give an adequate idea of the unaffected delight of the men. Timour maintained that the droppings are not more than three days old, and Iça declared that the partridge feathers also were quite fresh. Abdullah, after an examination of the sticks and the ashes of the fire, exclaimed that the men must be quite close.

Parpa alone was pessimistic. He urged that it did not follow that we should soon encounter men, for when shooting parties come out they often wander far away from all human habitations. He suggested that they might perhaps be watching us without our observing them. Still, he thought it a good sign, and as he could muster up a little Chinese, he managed to say a few words to the Dungan, whose chief entered quite amicably into conversation with Abdullah, whom he was going to kill only a few days before.

27

To me he exclaimed, "Adam, Adam!" (Man! Man!), and when I asked him his opinion, he was emphatic that the fire was not lighted more than four days before, and, moreover, that it was not lighted by lamas, as it is their habit, when they leave a fire, to disperse the stones.

When we had had our confabulation, we started afresh with a much lighter gait, and Rachmed, who went off in pursuit of partridges, which he heard calling to one another on the ridge of the mountain, came back to say that he had seen the site of another fire, while I observed an *obo* on one of the summits. It is clear that men come into these parts, and I believe we should find them if we went more to the east.

To-day we have seen monkeys crossing the frozen river and playing on the rocks which form its banks. But we cannot kill one of these animals, which are very short, with red hair, small head, and almost imperceptible tail.

We pitch our tents near the river, just at the issue of the defile through which it winds its tortuous way down from the Dupleix mountains, and not far from here, on the plateau, are the remains of a *yourt* of nomad Thibetans. This consists of four small ovens with very rough masonry, the fragments of a bag made of yak wool, the site of a tent with pegs made of *orongo's* horns, and the droppings of domesticated yaks smaller than those of the wild breeds. We catch sight of wolves, and kill some red-footed hares, which we eat. And all this—monkeys, hares, the *yourt*, the various tracks made by flocks, the plain which we are convinced we shall descry to the east when the snow ceases, the very snow, which is converted into excellent water; with the consciousness that we have descended to a rather lower altitude, and that the wind is not so strong—revives the drooping spirits of our men. Yet this night the thermometer went down to 48° below zero, whereas on the previous days the minimum had not been more than − 22°.

January 19.—This morning we get some lark-shooting and plainly see two valleys, one coming from the north-east and the other from the east, and converging at the point where we yesterday saw the monkeys playing on the river surface. At the foot of the mountain spurs, to the south of our camp, are some hot springs of drinkable water running over the ice, and in front is a level plain rising by very slow degrees to a tract of land, beyond which is a rather high mass of mountains. Fortunately, the presence of man in this region is beyond doubt, or else the view of this fresh range of mountains would have affected our men very unfavourably.

It is surprising to see, in the midst of this plain of hot springs, cones of ice, twenty feet or more in diameter, about the height of a man, and speckled over on their surface—which is just like crystals—with grit and stones from the plain; these blocks have split perpendicularly like certain kinds of over-ripe fruit. We have before us frozen geysers, which have become covered with this solid head-dress when their power of ejection was not sufficient to cope with the frost. We also come upon some fine roots of *iabshans* (?), which form very fine bunches, and with these we make an unsuccessful attempt to cook a *palao*.

We should much like to eat some of the rice we have carried such a long way, but it is impossible to cook it on account of the altitude, and our meat, of course, does not cook any better. It does not spoil, for it is frozen so hard that when we want to put a piece in the pot, we have to chop it as if it were a piece of wood, while the fat we eat for butter is as hard as a stone, and might be used as a projectile.

January 20.—The event of to-day is the discovery of the tracks of a horseman—tracks which are not new—and of a fragment of a saddle made in a particular way, which Abdullah says must have belonged to a camel. This suggestion is scouted by Parpa, who is a saddler by trade, and is not at all fond of the interpreter.

The merest trifles are fastened upon, as is the case with navigators
in search of land; but, while these are mere suppositions, we
have as certain facts that the west wind does not go down or
the cold decrease, the thermometer marking 27° below zero;
that we are still going up and down hills; and that our
animals are dying off very fast, while those which survive are
devoid of all strength. Our horses are incapable of the slightest
effort, and the camels are kept alive on dough and paste. The
grass peculiar to the highlands is hard and ligneous—like zinc—
and although the camels eat it, they are just as hungry as before,
so that it is necessary to hobble them to prevent them gnawing
their saddles. We have ten camels and seven horses left, while
the Dungan still has fourteen camels.

There are plenty of yaks in this region, but they are very
wild, and make off before we can get within fair shooting
distance of them.

January 21.—The Chinese New Year is celebrated with a
certain amount of form, thanks to a young stag shot by Rachmed.
Its flesh is so good that we eat the whole of it, first raw,
and then toasting slices of it on the *argol.* Iça is very
funny with his thigh-bone covered with meat, for he holds it
in his hand like a sceptre while he is talking. When he wants
to eat a piece, he holds it before the fire, tears off with his wolf-
like teeth the part which has got cooked, and so continues as
long as there is any left.

January 22.—The men's attention is attracted by large leaves
which prove to be those of the rhubarb plant, and yesterday
Prince Henry saw some edelweiss.

Numerous flocks and herds have lived in this region during
the summer, under the care of shepherds, for we can distinguish
the paths made in the soil between the encampment and the pool
where they were wont to go and drink, and they have left behind
them heaps of dung which we find useful for fuel.

RANGE OF ICY PEAKS (p. 201).

Around the old encampments we often see large crows, with a big and crooked beak like that of the larger birds of prey. They have very powerful claws, and instead of croaking like their European congeners, they emit harsh, cavernous, and vibrating sounds, like a lock that wants oil. This is why travellers have given them the name of " crows with a metallic croak," and though they doubtless are in the habit of coming to this place, we are evidently not the travellers they would like to see, for they nearly all make off after looking at us for a few minutes.

I need say nothing about the scenery, for it is always the same—first a pass, then a valley, then a halt near a lake, then another pass, and so on. We are still in a desert, but it is a desert which has been inhabited, and this makes our men much more cheerful, for they argue that the difficulties cannot be more insurmountable for them than they have been for others.

January 24.—Iça, on his return from fetching the camels, points southward, and says : " I have seen men in that direction ; I have recognised flocks of yaks and sheep."

Timour and Rachmed start off at once to verify this statement, and the west wind announces a change of temperature, for it seems moister than usual ; but as a hurricane of snow and dust sets in, they come back without having been able to see anything. This unlooked-for moisture, and the diminution in the size of the snowflakes, lead us to believe that there are large lakes evaporating to the west of our route, and charging with vapour the winds which pass over them.

Proceeding forward in these snowstorms, we came suddenly upon a frozen geyser about 33 feet in diameter, and then the sky cleared and we were surprised to see a large herd of several hundred yaks roaming along the sides of the mountain and feeding so quietly that we took them for domesticated animals, especially as we imagined we could see the shepherds looking after them. Having been able to get close to them without exciting their attention, we soon found that we were mistaken in thinking them tame, and when Prince Henry and Father Dedeken tried to stalk them, they made off.

This evening our people say that the Dungan would do well to remove the little bell hanging from the neck of his camel, as it might attract the notice of men. It was only the other

DISTANT VIEW OF THE "BINOCLE" LAKE (*p.* 201).

day that they were longing for the company of their fellows, but now they have a childish notion that they are being watched by invisible horsemen.

January 27 —The minimum on the night of the 24th, owing to the snow, was only 11° below zero, as against 31° the next night, but the west wind had fallen during the night, only to spring up again in the morning about ten.

On the 26th we scaled rocks 18,300 feet high, and, looking in front of us, could see as many mountains as from the summit of the Tash Dawan, when we arrived on the high plateaus. One of our men expressed surprise at there being so many mountains

in the whole world, to say nothing of Thibet. We came upon a
flock of crows of ordinary size perched upon some rocks and
croaking, just as the birds which are found near to the dwellings
of man do, so we are evidently near to human beings.

To-day (the 27th) we descend a pleasant little valley with a
gentle slope, and the presence of some rhubarb, dandelion, and
grass leads us to believe that this place must be quite habitable
during the summer. There are numerous paths leading to
abandoned encampments, and there can be no doubt that the
Thibetans come and feed their flocks here during the fine weather,
passing the winter in warmer or more sheltered regions.

We go cheerfully on, and as the sun is shining brightly, and
the wind does not blow in this little valley, we might imagine it
to be spring-time. Down in the bottom, we see running water,
and make a rush for it, finding it, to our delight, fresh and
good to drink. Along the slopes of this valley, there is grass
in abundance, while on a broad and sheltered terrace are great
heaps of very dry *argol*. We find that this stream is not frozen
because it is fed by numerous hot springs which are only
slightly salt, and it contains a quantity of small fish, whose
evolutions suffice to amuse us. Abdullah is in high glee, and will
have it that we are at the sources of the Brahma-Pootra, and
that all we have to do is descend the river and we shall arrive at
Lhassa. He is brimming over with happiness, declaring that we
have already made a journey which no one else has made, that it
is reaching its close, and that, for his part, you will never catch
him again in this accursed Thibet.

We cross to the right bank of the river, and, after going four
or five miles, find that, as its banks gradually get lower, it is
frozen over and ends in a kind of lake, on the ice of which the
water trickles until it has become solidified. While the tent is
being pitched, I go out to reconnoitre, and find that the river has
a very broad bed, but that it becomes lost in a rather large lake,

28

which it may possibly pass through after the thaw. On my return, Abdullah questions me, and when he learns the truth, his face grows very long, and he moans: " We shall never find our way through ! "

Nevertheless, the day is spent in rejoicings, for these parallel paths run in the same direction, viz., to the south-east, and they must form a main route of communication. All we need is to see men, in order to acquire the certainty that we are really on the road to the Namtso (Tengri Nor) and Lhassa.

January 28.—We continue going downhill, much to our satisfaction, about six miles to the south-east, and have to shorten our stages in proportion to the forces of the men and the animals.

January 29.—Last evening we encamped at an elevation of 15,700 feet, and to-day we are at 14,500. We get up a lottery to be won by the person who makes the nearest guesses at the date when we shall encounter the Thibetans, the periods selected varying from twenty days to four.

A WILD YAK.

END OF VOL. I.

PRINTED BY CASSELL & COMPANY, LIMITED, LA BELLE SAUVAGE, LUDGATE HILL, LONDON, E.C.